T0278263

series « cinema-fictions » directed by

DANIÈLE RIVIÈRE

in the same series

RAUL RUIZ
Poetics of cinema, 1
Poetics of cinema, 2
The Book of Disappearances & The Book of Tractations
In Pursuit of Treasure Island
The Wit of the Staircase
A Nine Year Old Aviator

PETER GREENAWAY
Gold
The Falls
Rosa
Fear of Drowning by numbers

BRUNO DUMONT
Life of Jesus
Humanity

MANOEL DE OLIVEIRA
Angelica
Lisbonne Culturelle
Les Cannibales

@ DIS VOIR, 2022
1 CITÉ RIVERIN
75010 PARIS
www.disvoir.com
contact@disvoir.com
ISBN 978-2-38162-006-0

Published with support from

FONDATION
JAN MICHALSK
POUR
L'ECRITURE
ET LA
LITTERATURE

RAUL RUIZ

NOTES, RECOLLECTIONS AND SEQUENCES OF THINGS SEEN

Extracts from a personal diary
Selected by
Érik Bullot & Bruno Cuneo

Translated from the Spanish by
Catherine Petit & Paul Buck

PROLOGUE

*T*owards the end of 1993, Raul Ruiz began writing this personal diary, which he kept until a few months before his death, writing every day, sometimes several times a day. At the beginning, it was simply a question of "reheating" or keeping a logbook of his days, making sure that the significant or "uppercase" facts, as he used to call them, always appeared diluted among the "minute" events of daily life, for he didn't want to give the illusion that his days were only composed of events particularly revealing, or of genial occurrences.

Gradually though, the diary became something more: a way to return to the Spanish tongue after many years in exile, to practise dialogue with oneself during periods of media attention – and even a literary experiment conceived to both rethink the conventions of the genre and to ponder them.

Between 2001 and 2002, for example, Ruiz wrote two, if not three, diaries at the same time with the purpose, he said, to explore the theme of the "consensual split-personality" and to always question what it meant to keep a personal diary which as such is not written with an eventual reader in mind, but whose author cannot either make abstraction of the fact that it could be read and eventually published.

This edition prepared by us focuses on the ideas, recollections and impressions that mainly deal with cinema and moments of thought in Ruiz's cinematographic poetics.[1]

Bruno Cuneo

*R*aul Ruiz's œuvre displays a vertiginous wealth of invention. As well as film making, he accumulated the activities of artist, writer (poetry, theatre, novel), teacher, theoretician, and all that with regularity, if not in a voracious fashion. How was such an artistic whirlwind organised? The reading of his *Diary* is enlightening in that respect, like a central laboratory. Written in Spanish, it accompanies the last eighteen years of the life of the cineaste, with the daily annotation of his impressions, his encounters, his readings. The *Diary* came up at a paradoxical moment in his career. Though at the time he was directing more ambitious productions, with famous actors and a new media coverage, he was no longer in the euphoria of the 1980s and their experimental magic. At times, the impression of capitulation comes to the surface. He carried on experimenting, of course, but his films were made in more difficult times of production and diffusion. As we advance in the reading of the text, we discover a profound and bitter-tasting melancholy, bound to the upheaval of the times, the laws of the market and the ageing process.

To this Saturnian mood corresponds, curiously enough, a conceptual joy whose expression is the *Diary*. Though the cineaste penned with care the progression of his projects (he enjoyed making lists and listing programmes) and pinned down new ideas for films, his reading notes are the spring board for theoretical hypotheses on

[1] Extracts from his personal diary published in Chile, 2017 (*Diario. Notas, recuerdos y secuencias de cosas vistas*, Édition, sélection et prologue de Bruno Cuneo, Santiago du Chili, Éditions Université Diego Portales, 2017 -2 vol).

cinema. The medium has become a manner of thought object, susceptible to "conceptual simulations", which enabled him to develop insights on, among others, the relations between the nature of the narrative and the production of an image (it is the nature of the images that determines the narrative, according to one of the principles developed in his *Poetics of cinema* 1), the construction and the structure, the theories of memory inspired by biology. Some propositions were developed in future articles and essays but others, and there are many, remain unpublished, on the edge of intuition. These rockets, at times sibylline, often dazzling, display an intense curiosity pulling out all the stops, hence the countless references (I quote in no particular order) to analytical philosophy, the Russian formalists, the poetry of the troubadours, musical composition and theology. Erudition is a speculative method, already manifest in the two volumes of his *Poetics of cinema*. Knowledge forms a landscape within which the cineaste performs short circuits, splices, inversions. Does the continuous flow of the *Diary* express, according to the Surrealists' proposition, the real functioning of thought? On reading it we witness the incongruous emergence of ideas, the sudden budding of theoretical hypotheses that outline a mental cartography, ecstatic and conceptual.

Érik Bullot

Bruno Cuneo, is a Chilean poet, a doctor in Aesthetics from the University of Chile, and a professor with tenure at the Institute of art of the Pontifical Catholic University of Valparaiso. Director of Raul Ruiz' archives, he is the author of a selection of conversations with the cineaste (Ruiz. *Entrevistas escogidas - Filmografía comentada,* 2013), his diary and a collection of his poems (*Duelos y quebrantos*, 2019).

Érik Bullot, is a French cineaste whose films explore the formal and poetic potentialities of cinema. He recently published *Cinéma Roussel* and *L'Attrait des ventriloques* (Yellow Now, 2021 and 2022). He teaches cinema at the École nationale supérieure d'art in Bourges.

1993

Café de la Bastille. Yesterday, I finished writing my first letter in twenty years. Today I'm starting this diary about filming, the first in 52 years of life. The reasons? None. Something has 'unblocked' (gallicism) in my head. Curious to see what happens when I go back on a moment in the day and let things past *reheat* (*calendarsi*, Milanese dialect), hour by hour. (*21 November*)[1]

***

Political justification. In the end, it's only about checking that the images in a film are not just accidental. (*26 November*)

***

I remember Pascal Kané telling me: "Your theory of objects" – *Cahiers du Cinéma* 1975 or 76[2] – "is not bad, but it's inapplicable". It comes to mind as I leaf through Croce's *Breviary of Aesthetics*. Borges quoting I don't remember whom: Croce's ideas are irrefutable and inapplicable. But isn't it what we might call "conceptual simulation" (and what some call "virtual thinking")? Consistent theories that are not bound to a coherent corpus of theories. They form a theoretical field showing, rather than covering, a given field (the beautiful, for example), with a fabric of theories that embrace it, that clothe it. (*27 November*)

***

I came up with a phrase that made some French people fume: "My films are footnotes to the books I read when I'm filming." (*27 November*)

***

In the evening, reception at the Chilean embassy in honour of Luis Sepúlveda, the Chilean writer and author of a best seller, *The old man who read love stories*. I will read it one of these days. The Brazilian ambassador literally kidnapped me and I found myself at the Brazilian reception surrounded by Lusophone intellectuals: chaos and good humour. If I have to believe what they said, all of them have

5

---

[1] Fragment of the first annotation in the diary, started when Ruiz was 52.
[2] Raúl Ruiz, "Les Relations d'objets au cinéma". *Cahiers du Cinéma*, n° 287, 1978.

seen all my films (I myself haven't seen all my films. For example, I've never seen *What to do!*). (*30 November*)

***

Melvil [Poupaud] arrived yesterday, nervous, overexcited, very pale. He told me that, a few weeks ago, at a meeting of the lobby (or mafia) of European producers which try to control film subsidies throughout Europe, someone had praised the last production of Paulo [Branco], that finally has achieved much success in Paris (with the public and with the critics), generating a very violent reaction in all its members. The producers, supporters of the cinema of producers, that "packages images following normal standards and criteria of marketing and mass production", were opposed to those in favour of the auteur cinema, that sanctifies the author-writer-director (Claude Berri, Amiralay, Besson, etc.). In a very short time the polarisation, that has been existing for quite a while in the USA, has reached Europe, but transformed into a doctrine, an ideology, whereas in the USA, the fluctuation of demand, the multiplication of new options, in terms of market, the invention of new forms of production has rendered this polarisation meaningless, for in America, it has never evolved into an explicit doctrine. In both cases, the creation of new forms, the discussions around the means of expression, the emergence of new forms of audiovisual that make possible other art disciplines, other re-integrations, remain marginalised. Cinema has already happened. Only in the States (and soon in Latin America) does cinema carry on inventing itself, reinventing itself. Independent cinema is not a movement of film makers (auteur politics), but of films. (*4 December*)

***

Rereading the beginning of this diary. The rules of the genre are starting to emerge. To write during the day, forcing oneself to pass the time, transforms the diary into a horoscope or a horrorscope. (*17 December*)

***

Today, I've read Valeria's [Sarmiento**] new script. More simple, very touching. I feel like making childhood films. Going back on *Un corazón de carne y hueso*[3].

** Chilean filmmaker, wife and editor of many of Ruiz's films.
[3] Title of a book of stories that remains unpublished to this day.

But Valeria has the gift of a simplicity connected to emotion. In the end, each to their own. (*24 December*)

***

Chronologies: Kodály, disciple of Domeny, disciple of Brahms, disciple of Schumann. Arrau, disciple of Krause, disciple of Liszt, disciple of Czerny, disciple of Beethoven. Cinema, on the other hand, tends to start from scratch. The history of cinema is contained and repeated in every film. But can one call history a series of events that never cease to start again? (*25 December*)

***

It's always strange how elements that, in the script, were connected "in a sequence" suddenly take shape in a situation and make it possible to take shortcuts. Yesterday, suddenly, it seemed obvious to me that the sequence of Katia's house[4], that was planned as a moment of narrative suspension, has turned into a break, drastically changing the rhythm of the film and making more bearable the morbid elements of the script. The problem is always the same: how to be able to anticipate with a little bit of time the direction from which new ideas are going to appear. All of these problems are unsurmountable in the new systems of production, in which any change remains outside the assembly chain and causes astonishment and anger. In the end it is about leaving creative spaces open to all, actors, set designers, lighting, etc., and connects them at the last minute to situations that are really new. (*30 December*)

1994

Very icy night. The cold makes images from three decades ago resurface: my first stay in Concepción, living in a monastery and writing day and night. I was 19 years old and had been given the most important scholarship a Chilean writer can aspire to[5]. Long wintery

7

---

[4] Character in the film *Fado, major and minor* (1993).
[5] It refers to the scholarship Taller de Escritores de la Universidad de la Concepción, that relies on the financial support of the Rockefeller Foundation.

nights reading Joyce and Dostoevsky. *The Eternal Husband*, more specifically, and maybe some evidence: that [*Fado, major and minor*] is my first film. At least it is the continuation of my first film, *La maleta*: the same heaviness and extravagance, the feeling of doing things for the first time: plays on several planes of action inside the frame. Impression of starting again, but also fear of going back on my track before dying. That said, not even a trace of sadness. My ideal in life: Kantorowicz's epiphany (from Panofsky): "Master of his masters, disciple of his disciples, friend of his friends, he loved life and didn't fear death". (*7 January*)

***

For the whole day, I mulled over the idea that *Fado, major and minor* is my first film, or at least the continuation of *La maleta*. That unfinished film followed me around for so many years, giving me the reputation of someone incapable of finishing anything (despite the fact that at the time I had already completed a hundred comedies, some short and some long). Why my first film? Like *La maleta*, things follow one another in front of the camera, in a completely different way than the way I had planned them. Like *La maleta*, it has to be a film which I had prepared with the utmost care, confronting technical, theoretical and personal problems. It doesn't take place in any specific space, yet undoubtedly it is very concrete. The camera movements are strange and almost simple. There is a perverse play on the *dated* elements. And here also everybody shows enthusiasm for the film, at the same time as they remain outside, as if the private space that is constructed, that they construct, was radically incomprehensible, yet familiar. I have to go back on the idea of "private space" as a rhetorical figure that has obsessed me for so many years. A space made of liturgical shifts in which each recognises himself and is at the same time compatible with the others and out of reach. The space that is reminiscent of Bradley (and the extreme idealists), that the world of the others is *by definition* (that is, rhetorically) illusory. (*8 January*)

***

In Duke's, I bought Schoenberg's *Theory of harmony*, solely to compare some aspects of my combinatorial analysis to his principles on seriality. It is a little bit absurd, because one can't get, within a sign in movement subjected to multiple directions (cinema), a combinatorial analysis as rigorous as music. And it's not worth it. What is interesting in theme seriality is the multiple and random ebullition of signs that tie to others, generating dreams and recollections. Alchemy more than Cabala. (*23 April*)

1995

What separates a children's author from a naive author? It is clear that in the way of building the bridge that leads to childhood, several strategies of introspection are needed: bridges, planes, boats. To go up the river of life like a salmon, by leaping, or simply to walk along the coastline. The narrative value of an image, however arbitrary it might be, is its burden of evidence, and evidence doesn't always depend on good sense. An image like the one in this story: a Northern city, floating in the sea, whose only inhabitant is an 11 year old girl. Then the narrative consequences of the image: the girl lives like any other child; she goes to school, plays, goes to bed in her own time, goes to church, snores, needs food. But she ignores that the rest of the world exists. The development: one day a boat passes by and she discovers her loneliness, she wants to die and a wave sweeps her away, but she's immortal. Finally, the solution: she was created by a sailor who had lost his daughter and who one long night, at sea, thought of her with a painful obsession and gave birth to her in the middle of the ocean. (*9 April*)

***

I heard that [Joseph] Needham always supported the government of the Republic of China (including the Tiananmen massacre) and that he admired Taoism. What is exasperating in the Anglo-Saxon sino-logists is the recurrent litany of lamentations on the claustrophobic culture, the permanent search for synchronisms between pheno-mena of distinct order (the six predictions), the *I* (change), etc. They don't see, they don't want to see, to what extent the game of life expands and breaks down and becomes endlessly fascinating. They cannot see the civilisation, the only one that invented an art of living many lives, of travelling without moving, of expanding beyond one's body, beyond the present (in Chinese one conjugates only in the present, but it enables one to feel contemporary of the past and of the future, reflecting in the game of mirrors that is the present). (*9 April*)

***

There must be a moment when the internal and external landscapes identify with one another, end up being the same. The so-called "mental landscapes", dreamscapes. It might be, but I find it difficult to think that the mental projections and the external signs of displacement, the external projections, cancel each other out. Only an intense practice of vision can make it possible to detect these points which, I'm sure, are real, exist and, above all, can be photographed. By this I mean that it is possible to conceive a cinematographic work made up solely of landscapes and "bridging" projections, in which contemplation and interpretation (the mental process) are indiscernible. (*22 April*)

***

I carry on going back to the ideas for *Poetics of cinema II*. After each allegory, a commentary should follow. That way, I will continue expounding on the ideas for *Poetics of cinema*. Practical, no? I try to explain – explain to myself – the way fictions function in a film. In what manner they are constructed to allow, increase, intensify the circulation of real and mental images. In *Fado, major and minor*, for example, there is a central theme, a situation: a young man accompanied by a little girl arrives at the house of an eccentric old man. One is adamant that he has written to the other, the other denies having received the letters, then admits to it. They talk about a woman. The young man calls her equally my wife and my mother. Usually the disconnected fictional elements should make the spectator switch off, so that when he turns away he might be able to see images which convey other explicit fictions but in suspension. Because the main enemy of the image is the narrative that subjects the images to narrated events, in which "contemplating them, seeing them" is superfluous. The constant solecism that leads to question narratively the image: "What does it want to say?" (*23 April*)

***

A few weeks ago I read a good part of Luis Oyarzun's *Diario intimo*[6], the complete work. Strange to read diaries while writing a diary. And that fastidious habit wins me over day after day. There's so much spare time in airports and restaurants. At the same time, the conviction that one has to preserve a tone "without qualities". Something that connects all the diaries that I read is "a taste for more". There's no time for elaborating, and there is the demand for reality. What would be produced when one lies to oneself in a diary remains to be seen. Lying to oneself, having promised before to give the diary to read to no one. But who is no one? Neruda, in *Estravagario*, names it: it is one of the fragments of Man. In the planetary system that is each person, there are wandering comets that are those Nobodies or Ulysses. Natives of Lisbon. Unless they form a planetary system, as the wanderers of space did before entering the system of Ptolemy. (*11 June*)

***

This morning, while out for a stroll, I asked Valeria if she thought with words and she replied that no, she thought with facts, *dramatic* facts. She constructs *daydreams*, dreamy states, as if they were concepts, organises various types of *what if* and reorders them until they are coloured with a recognisable emotion. In other words, she continually uses the *mnemosyne effect*. What does that mean, the *mnemosyne effect*? When we remember a fact whose intensity renders it distinctive, we sometimes have difficulties describing it, because the remembered fact lives inside or near elements that concern it indirectly. With such facts comes to mind a patch of sun on a table, the smell of a cigarette, the buzz of a fly and someone (but who?) saying: "I'd rather die than..." From all those elements, an

---

[6] A Chilean philosopher and poet.

evocation resurfaces: they invoke a past that, however, remains concealed. I remember that in Iowa in 1963, with Grínor Rojo, when we wanted to feel nostalgic for Chile, we drank German white wine (Liebfraumilch) and listened to Al Jolson. From some unforgettable films, nothing in particular comes to mind, save the unforgettable character of a scene, and not even that we manage to visualise very clearly. Recently I got it into my head that the *mnemosyne effect* is the aura of a film, that which makes it individual, un-photographable, giving it cohesion. (*26 June*)

***

Today, we start the ninth day of filming [*Three lives and only one death*]. The crew has accommodated themselves rather quickly to my usual change of direction, and my insistence in filming each scene in the right order, but they don't get used to my habit of not watching the rushes, they take it as negligence. On the other hand, the system is built according to: a) the script, and b) good acting. My problem is that from the very beginning, for more than 30 years, I consider the script and good acting as the main obstacles to the transmission of an especially cinematographic emotion. The French legendary habit of the "good *splice*" hasn't gone away. The heaviness (*les lourdeurs*) of French cinema can be for a large part explained by the mannerisms of film making.

In any case, Mastroianni has a seriously anarchic background that enables the systole-diastole that proves to be useful for the job of acting. I'll say: an actor makes a gesture to attract attention, to capture the gaze, he says "look at me" and as soon as one has focused on him, he's already closed himself to everything, and he's saying "leave me alone, I'm here for no one". And then the attention veers in another direction and the image *is looped* and one can move to something else. In that sense, Mastroianni is the best actor I know. (*21 July*)

***

Last night I had a drink with Danièle Rivière and Atom Egoyan, who's preparing a new film in Canada while he's making a heavyweight for

Warner. We exchanged points of view and advice. Each of us has a distinct idea of how to dodge the American system. Personally, I find that impossible, because in the end, it's a system whose concern is to please the audience and it's increasingly easy to foresee the reactions of the general public by using previews and polls, and the conditioning of the public has reached a point of saturation. Films are made for the public, to shock, insult or ignore it, but the idea that one could make a good film without thinking about the audience (in the same way as one can make a good watch that will carry on being accurate even though no one looks at the time on it) is simply incomprehensible. (*9 November*)

1996

*R*eading Yuan Hong Dao's *Pilgrim of the clouds*, from the 16th-17th century: "The poorer one is, the less sad death seems; the sicker one is, the less sad poverty seems". The day before yesterday, I finished chapter 25 of my novel [*Jamaica Inn*[7]], which is a quarter of the book. Each mini-chapter is a little time bomb that should explode ten chapters later. The combinatory system (ten themes that weave and unravel without respecting the chronology) is strict, but I think it doesn't impede the reading: a mosaic of short stories that are like synopsises of feature films in which I forbid myself, I try to forbid myself to make use of mise-en-abîme or story within a story. (*1 January*)

***

Three days ago, during an interview with Thierry Jousse, a kind of aphorism came to me: let's imagine the audience watching a film as it would watch a striptease, that at the same moment the dancer ends up naked, she becomes transparent and we can see her skeleton. The average spectator would say: "I think I got it".

13

[7] Unpublished.

Reading an essay by Paz on Saint-John Perse: "The only character in the story is a being without a name and without a face, half flesh and half dream". A good image to explain the nature of the cinematographic character.

Chile is not a country, it is a military camp. To be Chilean doesn't refer to a personality, but to a sexual perversion: seeking an orgasm by means of laughing fits. (*14 April*)

***

Yesterday, return to Paris. In the evening, dinner at Michel Ciment's house with a Korean pianist, his wife (an actress) and daughter (a violinist). Once again I got carried away by talking a lot and my impulse to entertain at all costs, an impulse that I don't experience when I make films. Someone told me that I should put more of my talking during dinners in my films and more of my films in the dinners. (*15 April*)

***

I have read some pages of this diary, trying to find the point when I begin to turn into a character. There is no such point: the character appears and disappears. Who is he? From what we read, we learn that he reads a lot (that's not sure), that he has an immense curiosity (he tries to hang on to that), that he suffers from a tendency to pose (exact, but what pose?). (*22 April*)

***

Last night Barbet [Schroeder], the American producer of *Shattered Image,* called. He is angry because he read a declaration of mine saying that my films attract between 6,000 and 10,000 spectators per country (which is optimistic).

For part of the night I mulled over the distinction between *structure* and *construction*. Construction is the distribution of the elements of the work. Structure is the logic that inspires the work. When both come into conflict, the work suffers. Wittgenstein. "Internal relation, external relation". (*11 May*)

***

For almost a year now, I've had regular inflammation of my lymph nodes. No one wants to see the cancer that I see. I'm not scared of it and I still want to live. I remember Kantorowicz's epiphany: "Master of his masters, disciple of his disciples, friend of his friends, he loved life and didn't fear death". (*25 June*)

***

Gradually I begin to settle into situations in which the instability of the space predominates, which is that *Time regained* (Proust), that old project, is starting to take shape, or soul. The first images appear: tableaux that come to life and generate other tableaux that "turn into objects", Sartre would say. And permanent movement of the characters inside the tableau. Shift from one movement to another. (*31 July*)

***

Came to mind a game that would consist in travelling towards the past on various genealogical paths (Western and Eastern, but also primitive). Applied to myself, it would give: Klossowski (but not Bataille), Borges, Dinesen, Le Fanu, Chaucer, Saxo Grammaticus, [–], Snorri Sturluson, [–]. Other possibilities: Neruda, Parra, Rulfo, Lezama, Calderon, Lope, Góngora, Juan Manuel, *One thousand and one nights*. Other possibilities: Bergman, Buñuel, Picasso, Van Gogh, Gogol, Swedenborg, Goya, El Greco, Velásquez, Cervantes, Castiglione, Saint Thomas, Avicenna, Ibn Arabi, Rumi, Zhuang Zhou, Democritus, Malinke songs. But there could also be perpendicular lists with various genealogies. And others. (*30 August*)

***

I gradually begin to put together a General Theory of Cinema (there are not many), which gives an account of cinema in general, of my work, but above all of the cinema of the future. Always according to the principle: in all fiction film, it is the image that determines the narrative, and not the opposite. But the question follows: what is an image? To which I reply: it is a figure made of the relationships between an object and another following a relationship container-content. Each visual unity has at least two objects in that relationship. The dynamic expression of such relationship creates a simple fact that reveals a simple relationship. Several facts form a set in which many simple relationships, progressively connected in a tree-like manner or as a trellis, generate vaster units. The development, the organisation of more complex images take place following two paradigms that alternate: the recursive and the narrative (strategic). The paradigm is used in the sense of Thomas Kuhn's, that is the set of unconscious habits or, sometimes, the model, the norms that preside over the development. The recursive paradigm means that the creation of an image from simple elements is made by ellipsis moving forward and returning in a cyclic way to the point of departure, but at the same time that global idea (strategic) is pursued, towards which it advances. I still have to figure out how this set of possible games comes about that include the final object.

Of all possible films, only one is the narrative model that we've known up to now (that of the central conflict). There are other possible linear models and many other interactive and many more made with combinatorial perspectives following conceptual simulations to be discovered yet. (*29 September*)

***

Yesterday, all of a sudden, I set out to write what I thought would be one of my regular poems and today, after five poems, I'm starting to realise that I'm writing a new collection. All that while reading with much pleasure a book by Wislawa Szymborska (the last Nobel prize). (*2 November*)

***

Three days ago, an explosion of creativity: 23 poems that put back together the pieces which my soul has been broken into over the last few months. At the same time, I begin to have theoretical ideas again, especially regarding the soundtrack. A curious theoretical fiction, according to which the micro-events that constitute a sequence must be imagined paired with sounds, in such a way that one can say indifferently that the sound surrounds the object or that the object surrounds the sound. Another idea is to imagine a system of elastic bands linking certain objects (a way of saying that there is tension between them). (*6 November*)

***

My idea is that the so-called artistic conventions are no more and no less valid than the rules of politeness. They are made to be broken. All poetic tensions are un-analysable because they are organisms structured on the basis of conventions. Conventions «clothe», conceal, the poetic body, but, if they are removed, the body evaporates. This explains why artistic works are unrepeatable and can only be copied. Parody is a meta-work, in the sense that it creates new tensions between the conventions put in tension and replicas of such conventions. The analysis of a work by elements and functions is meaningless. In the same way that dismembering a dancer's body will teach us nothing about her particular way of dancing. (*8 November*)

***

This morning I've worked on a poem, it's almost finished. After so many years trying to write poetry, it's happening. (*14 November*)

***

These last weeks I've been working on a book of poems (250 pages). The hard work is done. I give myself a year (God willing) to complete it. Almost all the poems are salvageable. They mark a return to Castilian and to myself. Otherwise, delirious sunsets, unpredictable hills and foreboding shapes. Of the wild figures, we don't know if they are mad, desperate or enthusiastic and foreboding. (Words are lacking more and more every day). (15 November)

1997

I can't say that I lack work: three films and two stage plays, a book and an installation. Too much. For the moment, my priority is the book of poems (*Duelos y Quebrantos*)[8]. (*9 January*)

***

Strange feeling of being on holiday. It's sunny, spring is coming. Reading Blanchot, an essay on Proust. He talks about the blending of time, the weaving of temporalities. To live is to remember. To remember is to see. To see is to revisit. To see again is to forget. To forget is to replace one memory with another. To replace is to yearn. To yearn is to foresee. (*7 March*)

***

Yesterday, after lunch, siesta and rewriting of *Fils de deux mères*. Later, music and a drink, and after, cinema: *Mars Attacks!*, boring and noisy. Tim Burton is a *gagman* but he's no cineaste. Not a single concern for the combination of signs: he loads and unloads without leaving any possibility to see, because there's nothing to see. The elements do not combine or separate. Disco effect. Valeria and I returned home in low spirits. (*11 March*).

***

Strange that my friends accept with so much ease my new situation as a high-profile film maker, read here, famous. (*21 March*)

***

Cloudy day, almost mournful. Conversation with Emilio [Del Solar][9]. At some point he told me: "*Time regained* is a mystical text", and that one sentence opened my eyes: it is the only thing that interests me in that book, which I've been reading with so much difficulty for the last 12 years, striving to find an equivalent in film terms. I stood up from the table straightaway and called Paulo, and in two minutes we agreed. It will be my next film. (*21 March*)

18

[8] An edition of 120 poems under this title was published by Bruno Cuneo in 2019: Raúl Ruiz, *Duelos y Quebrantos*. Viña del Mar: Mundana Ediciones.
[9] Chilean mathematician and musician living in Paris.

***

A malaise that gradually increases. Arrogance and counter-arrogance, sensation of having made a blunder. Of imposture. Undoubtedly media coverage is not pleasant. (*26 March*)

***

In the evening, I watched *L'exote*, still in editing. Much of the genuine tone, almost *amateur*, of the dialogues and the conviction of the camera movements hold. The story conveys an ironic theorisation: variations around the double, the theme of exile and the statue of Condillac. Two themes placed in tension: this has been my tacit rule for arranging my material with a film in mind. Its rule of unity. (*6 April*)

***

Pascal [Bonitzer] told me yesterday, unexpectedly: "Your friend Deleuze (he wanted to say the opposite) thinks that Proust, when he talks about time lost, was thinking about the time that passes pointlessly, and not about the good moments of the past". It could be called: *In search of tedium*. I add something that has to do with Portuguese *saudade*, which is the time for potential acts: nothing happened, but it was about to happen. I think about my reminiscences, that are themselves lost time but rest on the conviction that the act of reminiscing is a way to take action into the reachable, "without qualities" world of the past. This diary is my *madeleine*. (*8 April*)

***

Last night we had dinner at La Petite Auberge and discussed Michel Jouvet's theory of dreams: to dream is to bring our inner being into agreement with acquired experiences: dreaming is free will affected by determinism. (*14 April*)

***

Reading Michael Chekhov's exercises. All aim at unfolding the imagi-nation, but place the attention on the capacity to create transformations, metamorphosis. Of the type: "Look at a building. Then try to imagine it bigger, of another colour, etc. Think about a boy and try to age him mentally". Or "Imagine a little animal never seen before". (*17 April*)

19

***

At the Saint Amour, waiting for Silvia to sign the contract for *The Film to Come*(seven minutes) for the Locarno Festival. The starting point is simple, but the context can be complex: in a certain location in Belleville is the headquarters of a small, harmless sect, worshippers of a film fragment called *The Film to Come*. The protagonist has lost his daughter and looks for her among the members of the sect: a watchmaker, a restorer, an employee doing photocopies, a dealer in African art objects. They are, in fact, the four horsemen of the Apocalypse. After pursuits and intrigues, the protagonist discovers that his daughter is looking for him and that he is the one who's been taken by the sect. The end of the world takes place at every moment and the world is recreated at every moment. It is filmed in black and white as if it was a photo-novel: the characters holding poses while the rest of the scenery (people, falling things, etc.) moves at a fast pace. Make-up for effect, but done by me. (*25 April*)

***

I'm reconciled with [Walter] Benjamin. After having tormented me for a couple of years, his melancholic intelligence gradually imposes itself. I've been thinking about the medical examination for the insurance. They have found "unusual things" in my liver. (*27 June*)

***

Reading Benjamin, trying to develop his strange idea according to which the aura can be associated with the "unintended memory" (that of Proust). In cinema, no unintended memory could exist. We'll see. (*30 June*)

***

Frege's idea according to which a thought possesses an intuitive structure independent of language leads us to complete what has been said about the language of cinema, namely that the extensive articulations given by the rules of continuity are not necessarily compatible with the multiple weaving of internal relations that play with various articulations in a network, sequence or fabric made of motifs. (*17 August*)

***

I can't seem to be able to rid myself of a melancholy somewhat over-sentimental. It's true, I lost my desire to make the film [*Shattered Image*] and it won't come back except for a miracle. The manner of filming simply takes away all surprises during the shooting. There is no miracle possible. The smallest invention is eliminated before I even have the time to formulate it[10]. (*27 August*)

***

I would like to know what it is that compels me to carry on writing this diary. To know if that is what the readers call a "profound motivation" and, in that case, why I don't write more. At least it has been good for eliminating a slight tremor between the thumb and the forefinger of my right hand. (*27 August*)

***

I'm beginning to gradually enter *Time regained*. Valeria doesn't want me to do it, she thinks I am not equipped to do it and is afraid it would be used as a pretext by a lot of people who, according to her, would like to see me disappear from the audiovisual map. I don't know. I don't think it represents a danger for anyone (except for myself). (*20 September*)

***

This morning, a call from Chile woke me up to announce that I was awarded the Premio Nacional de Artes de la Representación y Audiovisuales. I'm delighted. My friends and family even more so. My mother said to me: "The emotion took away my appetite". (*22 September*)

***

Coming out of the cathedral, walking along the Rue des Frères, I came across an antique shop whose window display was beckoning me with a Dogon wooden statue. I went in and bought it (1,200 francs). It's great: a couple, husband and wife, embracing, sitting on a chair whose legs are naked young girls. The cashier asked me if I was me. Then he smiled and said: «It's very difficult to see your films, but I've seen several». (*8 October*)

***

From a certain point of view, I live in luxury. From another, I am the poorest of all cineastes. Poor rich. Spending all I have on books, music and restaurants. (*9 October*)

***

I went back to reading Cavalcanti's *Rime*. I picked up the translations of Confucius by Ezra Pound, and I started to deal seriously with *Time regained*. All of a sudden I have the feeling that I'm only doing silly things. (*12 October*)

***

The day is fresh and luminous. I feel that I've never left Paris with so little desire. I had only good news lately, which makes me feel insecure and plagued by anxieties of obscure origin. I feel guilty for everything. (*12 October*)

***

Yesterday I read a wonderful introduction to Persius Flaccus' *Satyres* by Bernard Pautrat. The distinction between intimate rejoicing and open laughter. (*18 October*)

***

Yesterday, between rancheras and Jalisco sones[11], I had the time to go over my life. A futile and sad task. Reading Persius Flaccus helped me though. This morning I read several pages of the chapter from the history of film theories devoted to Mitry and his refutation of Metz: cinema is not nor can be compared to a language. I feel like making an undecipherable film. (*19 October*)

***

As I left I took a book at random: Benjamin, *Écrits français*. An appropriate rereading in these times. This morning I woke up very early and with a physical anxiety that comes, I guess, from the exhaustion of travelling and from excesses. I read the runes, which predicted good things. (*26 October*)

***

The green of the ink brings back images from my childhood, when I was writing with my Waterman fountain pen. A strange backwards

---

[11] Popular songs (trans.)

turn, the fashion of pens as a reaction to the computer, the excessive customisation. Strange return of the hand (you can say that again) of the "inspired manipulation". (*30 October*)

***

Confusion of ideas and feelings.
Our profession, or art, is disappearing. Nothing's left of the enthusiasm of the 1960s for getting rid of an obsolete cinema. Today more than ever (including that which I do). There's no magic in our work. (*3 November*)

***

Not to fear Chile (the most difficult). (6 November)

***

Recycling the idea of Étienne Rabaud, an entomologist: «It is the individualism of ants that generates the geometry of their movements». Read: it is chaotic behaviour that generates symmetrical structures. Or: «The accumulation of chaotic facts creates symmetrical formations (crystals, stars, etc.), from which asymmetries must be extracted to make them fly towards the individual chaos of the beginning". It is not well expressed, but behind it there must be a rule of aesthetics: not to start from chaos towards symmetrical figures, but from original natural symmetries created by the game of dice (limited chaos) and to move them towards chaotic forms that highlights the importance of the symmetrical ossatura (simple structures). (*10 November*)

***

I woke up with the following idea. In most wide shots, spaces of different types coexist, which presupposes potential sequences, which the eye naturally makes roaming over the moving image, sometimes following a contradictory or complementary movement. This shift creates a mixture of centripetal movements towards what is important in the frame and centrifugal movements towards other possible frames within the frame, but far from the centre of the composition (knowing that the composition is produced by a series of movements, that favour convergence, and not by a series of volumes). A good movement should then weaken the centre of attention, so that it feels free to move around the frame. In order to achieve this, it is necessary to work with frames that, when confronted with others, provoke a shock. But how does the *hors-champ* work in this case? (*11 November*)

***

Yesterday, Valeria read the diary. I was upset because she started to interpret it. Every diary is a confession, even though it says nothing, because the non-said gives the impression of concealment. It creates a presumption of crime. (*11 November*)

***

The more I write this diary, which is a death certificate, the more I realise that because I never wrote by hand, I don't have a handwriting style, which is to say the movement of the nib doesn't know yet *the shortest route*. I ended up finding my T: T T T T T T T T! Yesterday Giorgio [Agamben] said in passing that because typewriters have disappeared from the world, he went back to writing by hand and that only at the end does he type it on the computer. (*12 November*)

***

While paying, I dropped a 20 cents coin. I picked it up with great effort and it came to me that it is how I'm going to die: trying to pick up a 20 cents coin. And that's because I'm plagued by the superstition that not picking up a coin is a sin. Taking hold of the money under the table, I saw that there was another 20 cents under the next table, but I didn't have the courage to pick it up. (*12 November*)

***

The afternoon ended with a desire to go out, to the cinema or simply for a walk and do nothing. Each time something makes possible my present success (let's not exaggerate, it is a very small success, relative, frugal, a kind of confluence of various lines), the more I feel hemmed in by my friends, who push me in that direction. Sadness and autism. I think that from today I'll go into hiding. (*15 November*)

***

I saw, a couple of hours ago, a few images from John Woo's latest film, *Face/Off*. Clever, but with the emphasis of cartoons. There is no justification whatsoever for the zombies of *Cahiers du Cinéma* to get overexcited (for dead they are). I don't know where that fascination of the French for American cinema comes from. In short, shallowness and greed for money, an abomination of imperialist origin. (*18 November*)

***

During the flight, in spite of fatigue, I carried on reading more than watching films. The person sitting next to me, on the other hand, must have seen at least three of the four films on offer. I didn't have the courage, I see all the mechanisms, the absence of any real imagination, the seductive elements, and a lack of generosity and faith. Instead of that, I had a good time reading Alfonso Calderón's *Memorial del viejo Santiago*, a few fascinating pages by Giovanni Macchia and even John Le Carré went down well. Less so the stories of Sheridan Le Fanu, despite the fact that gradually, that incredibly melancholic prose, which I liked so much when I was a teenage boy, sets in. An ideal writer to read on a heavy rainy day, sitting in a wooden tavern, beneath a swaying lamp, drinking mulled wine. (*19 November*)

***

I try to start reading *The varieties of metaphysical poetry*. With no success. I'm always struck by the emphasis Eliot put on technical issues and his scant interest in poetic enlightenment. He is one of the precursors of today's American *workshops*, which postulate that a poem is explained by its structure. I had no new idea for *Time regained*. (*23 November*)

***

My coming months, God willing, can be described like this: December: Paris, between the 1st and 4th: meeting with Grimblat and Clermont-Tonnerre and lecturing (2 and 3) in Le Fresnoy. On the 4th, travel to Chile. On the 9th, prize giving. On the 14th, travel to L.A. On the 18th, return to Santiago. Writing the script (scripts?). End of the year celebrations with family. January: on the 4th, travel to Paris, dubbing of *Shattered Images*, classes. On the 15th or the 20th, travel to Toronto. Mixing till 15th February. Return to Paris and writing *Time Regained* with the script writer and, in parallel, editing *Miotte*. March: on the

15th, travel to Hong Kong and completion of *Comédie des ombres*. April: on the 10th, return to Paris. Completion and mixing *Miotte*. In parallel, lecturing at Le Fresnoy. On the 20th, filming *La retrospectiva*. May: end of filming and beginning of editing in Le Fresnoy and Paris. June: I start the preparation for *Time Regained* (there doesn't leave much time). July: preparation for *Time Regained* and completion of *La retrospectiva*. August: filming of *Time Regained*. September: filming of *Time Regained*. October: filming of *Time Regained*, on the 20th, beginning of the editing. November: editing and preparation of *Fils de deux mères*. December: editing of *Time Regained* and preparation of *Fils de deux mères*. On the 15th, travel to Chile. January: on the 15th, filming of *Fils de deux mères*. February: filming of *Fils de deux mères*. March: editing *Fils de deux mères*. Preparation of *Navarro*. April: filming of *Navarro*. May: filming of *Navarro*. Cannes. June: editing of *Navarro*. Preparation of *Vertige*. July: preparation and filming of *Vertige*. August: filming *Vertige*. From there and all the way to 2000 (God forgive me), free of error or omission, which abound these days. I am still left with starting six films for television, two American films and, personal joy, the theatre play of Evelyne [Pieiller], and a Lope de Vega. And a couple of experimental films. And afterwards another millennium will come, with death the coldest and closest, if it's not there already. (*24 November*)

***

As the date for travelling to Chile approaches, I've begun experiencing a heavy and sticky anxiety that accompanies me everywhere. (*26 November*)

***

Listening again to *Ofrenda musical*. If one could find such a combinatory richness in a film. (*27 November*)

***

I go back more and more on the assumptions that lie beneath a diary like this one. One must tell oneself that someone is going to read it. One must establish that it won't be important enough to justify the curiosity of that person. But there's something else: there is the magic of the events that took place, magic in the fact that those traces left in the diary are even. Fascination of that near absence made into fragments by the omnipresence of chronology. Another thing is to go back on the diary, reread it and resist the temptation to correct it, to get rid of facts, things already mentioned, with the perverse pleasure of knowing one capable of assassinating blurred avatars. Those nomadic air bubbles. (*27 November*)

***

Alfonso [Varela] thinks that I am in a middle of a nervous breakdown. I am sad, period. (*2 December*)

***

The spectre of the disappearance of cinema is still coursing through Europe. And the most dangerous at that game are the Socialists (today in power) because they lack bad conscience. (*4 December*)

***

In the restaurant of the Hotel Le Parc, having breakfast, because for me it is 1.30 p.m. (cheese omelette and decaffeinated coffee), reading this time *L'idée fixe*. Memories of youth: Valéry's text was a recurrent element in our conversations, especially the whole idea of *implex*, that today I understand in a different way than at the time: in those years, the *implex* was for me a kind of multiple, sudden, intense potentiality in whose intensity the enlightenment rested. Today I understand it as a kind of virtuality that acts like the aura of the causal becoming. (*18 December*)

***

The narrative spirit is taking hold of me. The narrative paradigm, that series of automatic actions and reactions that quickly form an unconscious corpus that awakens each time the fiction is established and falls asleep each time the expression (the mythical) makes the fiction disappear. Thanks to the complexification of the structures, the linear fiction, because of the effect of multiple effusions, is stratified, becomes a landscape revealing the totality of the work. Again the appearance of the *implex* is responsible for that swarming of possibilities to have us forget the succession of facts with only two constraints (past and future) whose accumulation increases the interest. One can imagine that progression like a rushing towards a revelation of a vertiginous fictional field. Something like a cyclone in which the elements of the film, destroyed, fragmented in the middle of the whirlwind, are seen or perceived. (*21 December*)

***

Is a diary, from the very beginning, a text to be published? I think so. If not, why write it? But with one proviso: the presumption of innocence, the principle of privacy, not much different from Coleridge's "suspension of disbelief". (*23 December*)

1998

*M*y parents are getting old and each day is a challenge for them, a long journey towards the night. One more time I've assimilated and come to terms with the sufferings and anxieties of my family and friends. My friends are over 50 and contemplate with dread old age, poverty, and unemployment. I've rarely seen with so much clarity the world without compassion at this end of the century. The democratic distribution of misery. Result: two gastroenterites, a kidney infection and the reappearance of the infected fistula on which I was operated – and which I had forgotten – four years ago. Sadness, anxiety, solitude.
But I have reached the fifth chapter of a new detective novel. I've completed a third of *Time Regained*. A startling sun and the apotheosis of summer, with its scents and flavours.
I found in my room, in my parents' house, photos of *The statue*, my first theatre play, written when I was 17 and performed when I turned 19. Hans Ehrmann, who was a critic for *La Nación* at the time, considered it "the most promising event of the year". I find it hard to

believe, seeing the pictures and remembering it, that such a simple and unusual spectacle could have left such an impression that it encouraged me to pursue a career with no future, but so charged with eternities. (*3 January*)

***

I'm going back on the second part of *Time Regained*. I stopped the novel because I ran out of ink cartridges. Gradually the moment approaches when I will be forced to accept working on a computer. In the meantime, I do daily exercises in handwriting (this diary is part of it). *10.30 p.m.* In the plane, direction Miami. I finally managed to set up an account in the bank and I left several cheques to round off family finances. Apart from that, as usual, an intense sensation of the absurd. I had lunch with my parents and Juvenal Canobra: empanadas, lobsters and a stew. My father remains cheerfully delirious and rambles, except that there is nothing cheerful in what he's experiencing, he's simply losing control of his mental faculties. I understand the mood swings and the confusions that engulf him. In a certain way, I'm experiencing them myself.
11.30 p.m. Flying to the north of Chile. I changed seat. I read in *La Segunda* a heartfelt article by Mario Vargas Llosa defending parallel economy. He is right about the economical mechanisms, but wrong in the principles that support them. A kind of melancholy and nostalgia in which are mixed images of friends dying or recently passed away, burnt by the sun of this terrible summer, in which everything's going wrong for our dear Chile. (*5 January*)

***

It seems to me that in this film (*Time Regained*), music is the emotional undercurrent, as always, but also a narrative contrast, namely that the same music played in two scenes that apparently have nothing that relates them, connects them, and makes us discover a "film within a film". [...] One of the fascinating elements of *Time Regained* is the coexistence of different periods in the evolution of French society, not in terms of old and modern but as a system of vicious circles in which, simultaneously, a chain of facts can be in the past while another chain is in the present. (*12 February*)

***

I have come up with the idea of a diary in which the author spends a whole year trying to explain what he wrote on a particular day and gradually forgets to write down what is going on around him (except for futile facts, like the waiter's comments a minute ago, who asked how I could possibly write so tightly and so straight without having lines, to which I answered: 'Computers are worse'. (*12 February*)

***

Reading and re-reading Pound (*Sextus Propertius*). Hard, tense language. I'd like to film that way. (*22 February*)

***

This morning, I saw Valeria's film[12] [...]. There's something fascinating about that film. It begins like Chabrol, continues like Kundera and ends like Julien Green, in perplexity. (*23 February*)

***

The news from L.A. about the difficulties to find distributors for *Shattered Image* gave me a feeling of liberation, but it must have affected me because my sleep was disturbed. Again the spectre that says and repeats that my films are unsaleable, unseeable, indigestible. (*8 March*)

***

Ominous day in some countries (for us on 13 March, the day of Judas' treason). A little crestfallen but in good spirit. Suddenly I discovered that what made me distance myself from the world, from things, from myself and from my loved ones was the sudden loss of the *magic feeling*. That combination of pursuits and playful appropriations of the real world that make it at the same time, familiar and fascinating. It started with the appropriation of the studio in Le Fresnoy. There was a determining sign: Lille and Le Fresnoy are but one hour from Paris and I always went a little reluctantly, until I decided to take a suitcase, like someone undertaking a long trip. And suddenly I saw myself embarking on an adventure, as when, in 1960, I travelled to Concepción, overwhelmed by the expectations of a new life, fresh each day. That's how I felt yesterday, standing on my two feet, looking with a serene enthusiasm at the perspective of filming within a month.

---

[12] *L'Inconnu de Strasbourg* (1998).

Thinking with joy about my return to Paris and the perspective of going back to Le Fresnoy in a week's time. Wandering through the streets. What I'm doing is simply "re-enchanting the world". (*13 March*)

***

Yesterday I worked all morning, revising the poems that I wrote in Durham a year and a half ago. I wrote a Proustian poem. All these poems whose function is to connect, to link together my images, help me to *precipitate* the film's sequences: it is these images that determine the narrative. (*22 March*)

***

Yesterday my father's body was transported to the chapel of Nuestra Señora de la Divina Providencia, where we kept vigil all day (...). I woke up at 4 a.m. and mentally composed an eulogy from the words of the Muslim saint Hussayn Ibn Mansur Hallâj: "At times He gives you and in giving you He takes away from you./At times He takes away from you but in taking away He gives you,/ but when in taking everything away from you, He gives you everything/ it is perfection". (*3 April*)

***

I can't find a poetic subject that would be new to me and doesn't have a sense of pathos. Nothing that I haven't done earlier. So why should I be concerned by the fact that I have done something before and that I will go back to doing it again? But the problem is not the images or the articulations or the lucky finds. I think that when one begins a film, there should always be something that calls to mind the foundation of a city: the design and the maquette, but, above all, the sacrifice of a living being inside or outside the city. In this case, maybe my father. (*12 April*)

***

Sunny day. I went out for a coffee. I'm about to begin developing my new idea: *Entretiens avec les fleurs*. As always, associating micro-fictions with lists of objects. (*29 April*)

***

Last night I had dinner with Michel Snow and his musicians. Pleasant mood but a Canadian environment that reminded me of my dark hours in Toronto. Then I was approached by a Mr Jacotot, who had written a book in which he had gathered and put together all the cinema scripts written by people who are not film makers, scripts that were never shot. Now he wants to do an end of the century diary in which he attributes one space per person ("personality", he says), who has to write two pages. Ambiguity of the diary. Personally, I prefer a logbook. Telling the facts approximately and with a certain coldness, so that the accumulation is charged with pathos, but in this case it would make a literary work, though it might be by omission. (*29 April*)

***

On the train I managed to write a poem. I have to say that every time I say «write a poem» it's as if I were saying «I made a film»: the final editing and mixing are missing. (*8 May*)

***

I'm starting this diary again after having lost three others. All in taxis (and one in a train). With this it will come down to ten notebooks stuffed with notes, recollections and sequences of things seen. I pursue and persist.

(...) With the other notebooks have gone the chronicles of the build up to the most ambitious, the biggest, rather megalomaniac project of all those I had embarked upon till this moment: *Time Regained*. At this point, the project is going in the right direction. One month and a half before I start filming. The distribution is almost a joke. They are mostly actors who are talked about, at least in France, and I didn't even seek them, to be honest. A whirlwind of interest for everything Proustian has been generated. And I find myself, as always, without the necessary finance but with the most "important" budget a Latin American has ever had. (*27 September*)

***

Why do I persist in writing these logbooks that I lose so easily? Maybe what's happening is that I like the idea that they are lost when I'm on the verge of saying something that would compromise myself in my own eyes. Two days ago I read a sentence by Karl Kraus: "The artist turns the enigma into something evident". (*27 September*)

***

I've been in São Paulo for a couple of hours, and I've had the time to go over the first two thirds of *Time Regained*. I can't vouch for the level of legibility. For me everything is clear, because I've been living with those characters for more than a year now, but for a spectator who has never heard of Proust... It's clear, I think, that I have achieved something like the visual equivalent of Proust's style, and at the same time, a condensate of my own stylistic mannerisms. Everything I know how to do in cinema I've put in (and it's not little). At the same time, I feel that something's missing. (*28 September*)

***

It's getting increasingly clear that I will go back to writing. There are seven novels waiting to be finished. And many short stories and plays. One day there will be spare time for writing and reading. In a little while I shall concentrate on my daily poem. There are four hundred of them already. (*26 October*)

***

While I was having lunch, I thought of a story (reading Alain de Botton's beautiful book, *How Proust can change your life*): a man on the verge of suicide dreams that he is dying and sees his funeral and mourns. The dream is repeated several times until the man ends up getting used to the idea of dying every night. The dream, the certainty of dying at sunset, brings him back to life. He sees life with new eyes. He becomes optimistic. Until he discovers that he is actually dead and that he dreams every day that he is alive and that he is doing what he has not done in his lifetime. (*4 November*)

1999

*F*or a long time now all my films have had a hermetic component: behind the explicit elements hides a second, clandestine film with which the explicit film has no further dealings. (*21 April*)

***

I have the feeling that exhaustion settles in my body as if it meant to stay there forever. And the small pain in my right side comes and goes. Nothing to be done, the pain keeps coming and takes up my attention. (*19 May*)

***

Yesterday I re-read Oliver Sacks' book *An Anthropologist on Mars*, especially the chapter on the man who regains his sight and doesn't understand what he sees. An idea for a film: *The House of the Blind*. In an asylum in the 18th century, a group of elderly people undergo cataract surgery. They all recover their sight, except for one, who becomes the dictatorial and implacable leader. (*10 June*)

***

I began writing a couple of sonnets and ended the day making notes for a future film, to be made in Chile, that would encompass *El ideal de un calavera*, *El loco Estero*, *Martin Rivas*, *Los trasplantados* and *Umbral*. A very big tele-novella in which the history of Chile[13] would be covered. (*14 June*)

***

Yesterday I made inroads with the Chilean project [*Cofralandes*]. I started to make games of objects and situations. For example, can one say that the relations between the possibilities of association of functions are comparable to Wittgenstein's language games? Example: the water is turned off and people, having been informed beforehand, start filling receptacles with water. First the obvious ones: the bath tub, sinks, pots. Then the unusual ones: soup bowls, ashtrays, etc. Then relationships are established. The water is cut off

34

---

[13] This project was the last prepared by Raúl Ruiz in April 2011, four months before his death. The works mentioned are by Alberto Blest Gana and Juan Emar, Chilean writers.

and it rains and the light is cut off and candlesticks and candles are associated with receptacles filled with water and all that with a birthday party. (*24 June*)

***

I'm starting to give shape to the Chilean film [*Cofralandes*] and another big project around *One thousand and one nights*. It's obvious that digital video opens possibilities for that gigantic project: a narrative, a galaxy of narratives, that take as starting point *The tales of Kordofan*, the archaic version of *One thousand and one nights*, the political version. A project of a very large scale like Pound's *Cantos* or *Das Kapital*. A critical and poetic synthesis of our times. In the stories of *Kordofan*, a storyteller destroys, with his stories, the theocratic system that rules over the actions of men according to the movements of the stars. In our world, celebrity and money. In short, abstraction makes us forget real life. Fiction (which is unreal, but which is in contact with reality in many ways) can save men from the new theocracy of macroeconomy. It sounds naive, but it is a poetic plan, not a political one. Poetry operates by hiding what's evident and making manifest the intangible and the concealed. (*27 June*)

***

I bought Truman Capote's first novel, that I'd read 35 years ago in Santa Fe[14], living in Modesto Urteaga's house, which for the most part resembled the scenes in the American Deep South described by Capote. The novel can easily be broken into themes, which would give a cinema not much different from mine (I go from details to wide shots, evocations, five stories organically connected to the main story – for example, the ball that Joel steals in the lorry and which, with the feather of a blue bird will be the two main elements of the future collection, but which, at the same time, are reminiscent of the first collection of objects that compel him to leave New Orleans, etc.). (*3 July*)

***

I'm reading an interview with [George] Lucas in the *American Cinematographer*. He proposes, no more no less, the conversion

35

---

[14] In 1963, Ruiz took classes in cinema at the Instituto de Cinematografía de la Universidad Nacional de Santa Fe (Argentina).

from celluloid to digital. The advantages are obvious: a radical reduction in costs and the number of technicians, the democratisation of independent cinema. The disadvantages also: concentration, in the hands of a few (in one) of the control of the means of production, disintegration and an even greater dependence for the Third World countries, dehumanisation of the elements (it's no longer photography, language of the world, but a system of interpretation of numerical signs), and location shoots reduced to a minimum. (*7 September*)

***

Reading Eliot's *The Four Quartets* helped me find some serenity. It's strange that at 20, when I was most interested in the problems linked to infinity, I didn't see the connection with the poem. (*27 September*)

***

Recapitulation: I spent three weeks in Chile. I filmed a dozen hours for a documentary and, parallel to that, in the mornings, I wrote the new script for *Fils de deux mères*. We are starting to film in three weeks' time. My mother is well. Friends, not in great shape, but surviving. I rediscovered the country, filmed many landscapes. I read a little but, above all, I suffered from a pain in my left leg: gout, sciatica and rheumatism, the whole peppered with a decline that I ignored, but fought with a kind of grudging good spirit, very much our way. I take it easy but then I go out of my way with a drive for achievements that exalts me and carries everything. And I survive like that: four films to come (more like five), one after another. (*10 November*)

***

I carry on living in a mixture of euphoria and exhaustion, regretting not having the time to write more things, for example, more novels. (*5 December*)

***

For five years I've been writing poems, constantly. I'll gather them in folders of various colours. The time for a minor recapitulation is approaching. (*7 December*)

***

I had fun imagining how an American would have produced the script [for *Comedy of Innocence*]: Isabella would be bad and Ariane would fight with all her strength to defend her son, victim of a diabolical plot. Instead of that, Ariane ends up involved with Isabella, almost wishes that the fantastic hypothesis is the truth and the boy is the big manipulator. No one is punished and everyone ends up with the feeling of having lived "a strange adventure". (*14 December*)

2000

*Y*esterday afternoon I saw the first part of *Mr. Arkadin*. It has been five years since I've seen it. I liked it better. One perceives his disregard for the public because the film has little interest for an intrigue (a problem I'm familiar with) and especially because there are no attractive characters, only a situation in the form of a vicious circle. In a certain sense, one can take it as an allegory for the Inquisition. (I want to know everything about X, except that I myself am X). (*2 January*)

***

Again, I let myself be taken in by combinatory magic. It is definitely an art in which the magic of the Renaissance is to be found. (*1 March*)

***

I carried on reading Pessoa's poems and each time I feel more and more that I could have written them myself. (...) Finally, I made a film [*Comedy of Innocence*] that endorses the ideas I expressed in *Poetics of cinema*. (*2 March*)

***

The filming ended in applause. I think that I begin to see the end of the film. A curious film, it surprises me that the system of combinatory filming works so well. On the condition of knowing how to let go when it starts to be tyrannical. This morning I spoke with Valeria to ask her to do the editing of the film. I need the eye of someone like her: critical and loving. (*5 March*)

***

In my film there are details that don't lead anywhere. One can say that all the initial fictions don't lead anywhere while the fictions that are produced by the friction of motifs *reveal*, in the sense that they bring to light, hidden themes, as if cooked, heated by friction (cannibalism, for example). That film, made a little hastily, must be the most ambitious I have made. (*5 March*)

***

Last night I discovered that you can shoot video without changing the rhythm of life (family lunch, morning walk, reading). (*20 March*)

***

Last night, before dinner, the attaché took me to a meeting of poets. The place, the light, the way they were dressed, the faces, the attitudes of the attendees took me back 40 years to Chile. I saw the same poets, writing the same kind of poetry. The same audience. I even recognised old comrades from Bohemian days, and studies. I'm sure they talked about the same things. Only on the way out, looking at the cars, did I realise that I had seen wealthy spectres, the prosperous ghosts of those rat-poor poets that we were and who spent entire nights reading, talking and drinking beers served with spicy bread. (*22 March*)

***

Discussion about a Cassavetes film, which they criticize because of the absence of structure. I quote the distinction Florensky makes between *structure* and *construction*: the structure is the logic, the expression, the soul (the driving principle) of a work; the construction is the conjunction of the means that one takes – distribution of materials, balance, precautions – so that it doesn't collapse or disintegrate. There are connections between *construction* and *structure*, but one can say that the structure is a challenge to the construction. (*3 April*)

***

It is difficult to make people understand that cinema is always poetic, in the sense that it displays an evidence whose vertiginous undercurrent one has to see. One must reverse Coleridge's proposition: "suspension of disbelief" with "suspension of audibility". Creating facts that are paradoxical, self-referential, absurd, oneiric, while using familiar elements: objects of everyday life. (*4 April*)

***

I am gradually settling into the preparation of *Strong Souls*. I started to make a list of exercises for Laetitia Casta. In the evening, dinner with the producers. The rest of the day will be spent doing nothing (that is, preparing for future films). (*5 April*)

***

Last night, I had dinner at the home of Guy [Scarpetta]. The Robbe-Grillets were invited too. At some point, I got distracted from the conversation and heard Alain say: "There's no dead but there are several wounded and disfigured". I thought he was talking about a traffic accident, but no, it was about the trees in the wood around his château. We talked about the reason for writing an intimate diary when it is quite possible that it will end up being published, which forces one to improve the style and say things destined to a third party (that's not my case). I told them (but no one was listening to anyone) that, in my case, a diary is used as an *aide-mémoire*, but above all, because it gives to everyday life the character of a journey, of a voyage. Wandering, the natural way in which life presents itself, takes on the meaning of an investigation, or a quest. (*9 April*)

***

Tomorrow morning I have a gruelling press conference to present my *Poetics of cinema [II]*, that I already regret having published. Nothing in it is evident or amusing, it's pure vanity. Reaction of a young pup. But now the deed is done. (*7 May*)

***

Last night Andrés Claro[15] came for dinner. I prepared a tarragon chicken in white wine, saffron and summer truffles. It was good,

39

---

[15] Chilean philosopher living in Paris at the time.

accompanied by a Côte-Rôtie. We talked until 11 pm. Peaceful night. I dreamt I was making a film of raw meat slices. (*21 July*)

***

This morning I filmed for an hour and after I started to go over some papers: the dialogues of *Mille et une nuits à Belleville*, *L'autel de l'amitié* as well as the notes for my classes at Duke's. It still seems to me that the three theoretical problems that I propose at the beginning of the seminar remain valid, at least for me: A) Involvement and detachment. B) Specificity of the cinematographic emotion. C) Combinatorial analysis. (*24 July*)

***

There are four types of cinematic shots: 1) Centripetal, which attract images and provoke events. 2) Centrifugal, which push truncated events towards other shots, where they will be completed or push other events out of there. 3) Holistic, which concentrate in an allegorical form the totality of the film. 4) Those which are linked to others in terms of totality, which are parts of a finished game. These four functions can coexist in a single shot. (*31 October*)

2001

A novel-poem dictated into a tape recorder in 1926 (?) (I have the first edition, from 1929[16]). I recovered the images and atmosphere from readings in my youth of *Moravagine* and, above all, of *Trans-Siberian*, which I read and reread on night trains in the south of Chile in the 1960s. On the first page, Cendrars alludes to the mythical bar where there was a cat orchestra, in Castro, Chiloé (the Por Qué Pepita?). The style is much more tense, more intense, than in the later, better-known novels. There is an exhilaration shared by other writers of his generation (Apollinaire, Huidobro, Savinio), which again gives a taste

[16] He refers to *Confessions of Dan Yack*.

of youth. A permanent youth, which takes me out of the depressive tone of my recent Chilean readings (with the exception of Jorge Teillier[17]). (*19 January*)

***

I went out in the morning to retrieve two copies of *Documents* (1929-30) and found the bookshop closed. I went into the bookshop next door (a new Italian bookshop) and found a beautiful edition of Giordano Bruno's treatises on magic, including *De vinculis in genere*, which I had been seeking for years and which I had read with difficulty from a photocopy made at the Catholic University of Milan. I also bought a volume of novels by Alberto Savinio and two studies on Frederick the Swabian and the Sicilian school of the 13th century. By the time I left, the Librairie Fourcade had opened and I was able to retrieve my books, but I was already in a whirlwind so I bought two original editions of Supervielle, one of Tristan Tzara, Jacques Vaché's *War Letters*, etc. I went back home and cooked myself some lamb chops with a tomato salad. I spoke to Valeria and Paulo on the phone, then went out to buy more books in Vrin, this time on Port-Royal, *Chance and Rules* (L. Thirouin) and a series of studies on Nicole, a Jansenist scholar, author of a famous moral booklet, *The Prism of Morals*. I bought four cigars for tomorrow (a present for Waldo [Rojas][18]) and set to work on a double combinatorial system to deal with Port-Royal on film. One dealing with situations (the vertigo, the miracle of the holy thorn) and another dealing with power groups (Jesuits, Jansenists, libertines, La Fronde, etc.). (*27 January*)

***

Last night, insomnia and reading of Breton's *Communicating Vessels*, and, especially Philippe Soupault's *Journal d'un fantôme*. The diary of his return to France after the Liberation. Echoes of what I experienced in Chile. (*14 February*).

***

In a conference given in Basel (1870) about Socrates and the death of tragedy, Nietzsche declared that "most of the creative schemes have for a basis that creativity is unconscious and that reason serves as a dissuasive control for the events that emerge from the shadows.

---

[17] Chilean poet.
[18] Chilean poet residing in Paris.

On the other hand, for Socrates, creation is the fruit of reason and it is the *daimon* that is dissuasive." I started to think that the creative process is situated between the two models: intuition (dark and emotional) of a structure inhabited by ghosts and demons that make it habitable for them (dissuasive critic) so that after, the reason (discursive) expels these demons and makes it habitable for those who are awake (Apollonians). And then, like a cycle, the house is occupied, by day, by the Apollonians, by night by the Dionysians, until things reverse, and the Apollonians come to experience sleep while the demons of Dionysus venture into the light of reason without fleeing to hide in caves. There, in that moment, the work begins to live. Valéry: the classic artist constructs, the modern creates by causing accidents; the classic creates expectations, the romantic (modern) creates surprises. (*15 February*)

***

This morning, after coffee, I randomly opened the first volume of Simone Weil's *Notebooks* and found: "Not to read, to read the non-reading. Supreme art, order without form or name. Negation of form in great art. How to do this? By analysing...» (Plon, p. 103, 1951). (*17 February*)

***

Last night, dinner at home. I cooked a perch, loosely following Kharman's recipe: fish with redcurrants and raspberries in champagne, marinated in lemon and balsamic vinegar, breaded with almonds and drizzled with liquid honey, cumin, cinnamon, cloves and (new) tarragon and mint. (4 March)

***

I read a couple of folk tales compiled by Afanasiev that have once again left me in a state of perplexity. I tried to get into Larronde's *Les barricades mystérieuses*, without quite succeeding. The mystery persists. Then I turned to the prologue of Jacques Vaché's *War Letters* and got lost in meanderings. Then I went on to look at some reproductions of Paul Klee with the same results. Finally I started drawing and felt better. (*12 March*)

***

It's the first time I'm trying to write a notebook parallel to the one in which I write every morning at my desk. It will be my itinerant notebook, the one destined to be lost, the one written with a loose hand and with something like anti-melancholic slovenliness. (*12 March*)[19]

***

Some images for *Cofralandes*: a series of interiors that culminate in close-ups of details (an object), which leads us to another interior, until from detail to detail we find ourselves in a rubbish tip (or in a shop) where there are other objects glimpsed at in other interiors. Each object tells its own story. The history of a salt cellar: salt shakers, salaries, salt rites. Ashtray: ditto. (*13 March*)

***

This [*Strong Souls*] was the film of resignation. Just like *Love Torn in a Dream* was the film of enthusiasm, *Comedy of Innocence* the one of wit, and *Time Regained* the one of hope. Let's see the positive side: in this film, nothing worse than what was predicted can happen. (*15 March*)

***

"The Chilean looks, in general, native-like, with a shifty demeanour, shy, given to flattery, always a thief and an assassin when he feels so inclined." I got it in my head that it would be a good start to the second part of *Cofralandes* (see the parallel diary-notebook, suitably named "the Other"). (*15 March*)

***

Preparing myself for what's coming my way: disasters + disasters, all that in the middle of a good period, very strange. I've never had such a good time and I had never given in so easily to melancholy. (*19 March, PD*)

***

Going over the general principles of my poetics: the image determines the narrative or six functions of the frame. Recursive and strategic models. Industrial narrative paradigm, etc. (*25 March, PD*)

43

---

[19] From that date Ruiz started to keep a parallel diary – of which only two notebooks have been kept – without abandoning the writing of the main diary. The annotations corresponding to those parallel notebooks are here designated with the letters PD (parallel diary).

Regarding the most profound form of symbolism, Whitehead talks about the perception of the external world, the act of deciphering an object (a chair, for example) instantaneously and the fact that the effort of the artist is to *delay* the act of deciphering. I can think of the following case: we take a series of objects which can be taken apart - a chair, a table and a mannequin – and in quick succession, we assemble them and take them apart. To each fragment we attribute a musical sound. To each assembling and dismantling correspond musical assembling and dismantling. "Symbolism plays an essential part between our psychological functions in the way that it comes from our *immediate conscientiousness*" (hard fact). I think that the illusion or trap that is cinema, "that mirror with memory", has as basis the mechanisation of the register of the image, while that register is subject to idealisations and abstractions, like the absence of colours or framing. (*26 March, PD*)

***

Reading the book of Robert [Guyon], whom I will see at about 12.30 p.m. Very interesting. Introspection in the manner of Benjamin Constant, but at the same level, interspersed with poems. Introspection of the introspection. Mirroring unfolding until mirroring begins to fulfil the function of a meta-verb, meaning mental cinema. Glauber Rocha's dream: to film the interior, not the current of thought, but the immobility of the flow and the fluidity of the immobile. «When you move, like water / When you stop, like the mirror» (quote from Fung Yu-lan). (*7 April*)

***

Stéphane treated me to the latest book by Rosenbaum on the manipulations of Hollywood to prevent certain films that don't correspond to the norms of fabrication being known to the public. First argument: that someone needs thick clothes in winter is an obvious fact. It is less obvious that the public needs films each time more childish and digestible. Second: what the public asks doesn't always determine what's on offer. For example, the public asked for the free world to be protected against communism during the Cold War. Today it no longer asks for that, but the army carries on arming itself. (*11 April, PD*)

Yesterday, I had a few ideas for the editing of *Cofralandes*. In this film I'll be able to play at least with seven functions of shots: centrifugal, centripetal, combinatory, holistic, allegoric, critical, trellis. Maybe eight if we add the *twinnings*. (*12 April, PD*)

Yesterday, in a small Portuguese restaurant in the neighbourhood. Family clientele, what in Buenos Aires is called a «family bar». All painted green, but rather Chilean green than Portuguese green. I ordered a glass of Vinho Verde and then half a bottle of Periquita. Sardines and cod Portuguese-style.

I had brought Poe's *Extraordinary Stories* to leaf through during lunch. If I had known I was going to eat here I would have brought Pessoa. Over the years I've become increasingly fond of discreet synchronicities (and secret diachronies). This morning I read a few pages of *The Pan trilogy* by Jean Giono. The affinity with Juan Ramón Jiménez is evident. (*15 April*)

Gradually understanding and repeating to myself that, just as books fit in a library, the libraries that hold ideas and imagined facts are made of time. The Internet, intervening in time, occupying it, unfolding it into expectations (expected time) and realisations (fugitive time), distances us from the real time in which we live. (16 April)

We had dinner in a Cantonese restaurant with Linda, Hector and a stammering, nice young videographer. Then they took me to a shop to buy a new video camera that is almost as light as my Sony camera but with several advantages. Among them, built-in sound, which is becoming a necessity given the cost of technicians in Chile and the rest of the world. Hector thinks cinema is over and I think it's just beginning. (*22 April*)

Returning from Hong Kong, I arrived Monday 23rd. Bank transactions, calculations for payment and editing of *Cofralandes* which for now will be called *Cofralandes (Chilean Rhapsody)*. Gradually the images are coming together, forming the film they are part of. Cold and rainy days. The worse year since 1973. In the end, the film is more lyrical than creative. More Pound and less John Dos Passos. More subjective and less dossier. (*26 April*)

***

Yesterday Javier [Ruiz][20] arrived with a Manchego cheese as a gift. He spoke with great emphasis and then more affection about the hidden Syria, «of the thousand and one religions». He gave me a talisman and I gave him an ancient coin with Trajan's profile. We talked about the diviners of books, those like me, like Lezama Lima, according to Javier, take pleasure in imagining the whole book, sometimes after having read three pages. But that fame is double-edged, it's a way of saying «poets are not serious». The truth is that after reading ten pages (sometimes I read up to six books at the same time), the diviner reader plays at combining read facts, postulations and opinions, until devising something like a ghost book. Those pages read, often memorised (for example, I can quote the first sentence of Bruno's *De vinculis in genere*: «He who wants to operate with reality using links should have, so to speak, a universal theory of things in order to be in a position to overcome Man who, of all things, is the recapitulation of them...»). I have just read a story by H. C. Andersen. (*27 April*)

***

Cofralandes is going to be, of all the films I have made, the most *premeditated*, the one in which the non-narrative functions of the shot, its unconscious structure are favoured. (*30 April*)

***

Curious feeling of having two parallel diaries, though the other is simply called *"Notebooks"*, giving me the impression that one is throwing the ball to the other. It seems to me that they detest each other. This one, the oldest, doesn't want to know anything about the other, the red one which, like all youngsters, wants to get noticed. (*1 May*)

[20] Spanish archaeologist.

***

Sunny day in Paris. Yesterday we had lunch with the Rojas and Andrés Claro. Family atmosphere, friendly but a bit confusing, as if there were secrets or things implied. Then a heavy siesta and in the evening I made myself some lentils and read a few pages of the second book of *The Origin of all Religious Worship* by Charles Dupuis. The second volume is essentially devoted to explaining and defending, with poetic arguments, pantheism as a current of thought that has come from Egypt to the present day. The idea that nature has in it the impetus, the force, the principle of animation, of creation. «God is here», says the Christian hymn. It attacks the idea of the distant God, the absent creator, and replaces it with the idea of the God who has invented himself as he moves creation forward. Impossible not to associate it with the reading of M. de Chazal and his curious statement: «God is a receptacle of forms». Then, this morning, I went on to read, reread, except that I couldn't remember anything, J. W. Dunne, *An Experiment with Time*. His idea of the «train of images». There would be much to think and write about his claims and doubts. Something that has a lot to do with cinema. (*4 June*)

***

An idea that came to me in the car: in a bookshop, a game with hunters of first editions. An intrigue made up of an interweaving of searches, serialities. One book with another makes up a third book. Secret codes. The total book. Let's say, the cabala according to Ramon Llull (again). (*8 June*)

***

A man is born old and as he grows older he becomes a child. Another man is born a child at the moment of his death and grows old towards his birth. In the middle of life they meet and greet one another. And if they don't greet one another? (*10 June*)

***

Yesterday was an erratic day. Not done anything concrete except for wandering through the streets under the rain and reading a book by François Schintz, professor of logic at Nantes. A good summary and an excellent re-formulation of the theory of *Bild* in Wittgenstein's

Tractatus. Concerns of my adolescence and the origin of my ideas on cinema. (*14 June*)

***

In the *Cahiers de l'Herne* on Pound there is a good essay in which the ideas of Pound, Fenollosa and Eisenstein are put in parallel: an ideogram is composed of signs that refer to things and all these things put in relation form a concept. But what about the opposite path? An abstract fact, let's say rhythms and melodies in the melopoeia of a flute, dictates a concrete object, a Persian tapestry or the image of a shovel and a bucket (as Bruno Beaugé told me). (*8 July*)

***

As planned, we had a hearty lunch and I spent the afternoon reading Unamuno: the prologue and the first of the *Three Exemplary Novels*, where I think I found an idea for a film in Spain. A barren widow asks her lover to marry and have a child and to give her the child. In the «Prologue», Unamuno alludes to a certain Oliver Wendel Holmes, who, like myself, divides each character into three: 1) The one created by God (or the author). 2) The ideal of himself, or the character. 3) The ideal of the one who deals with it. Unamuno divides that in four according to the type of will: 1) The one who wants to be. 2) The one who wants not to be. 3) The one who does not want not to be. 4) The who does not want to be. But the Americans, by limiting the will to wanting «something», spoil the game, because one cannot want to be something and want to be something else. (*23 July*)

***

Valeria and I had lunch in an Italian restaurant and then we went for a coffee and reminisced about our childhoods. Valeria went to work, the wind is gathering and it's getting cooler. Thinking, as usual, about what films to make. In front of me, a square. I've had a hard time getting back to some ideas for film. At 5.30 p.m. the antiquarian bookshop opens. (*26 July*)

***

Two days ago, in the Kurdish restaurant, I met Chantal Akerman, who was about to go to Mexico to film a documentary about *nothing at all.*

We stayed up late talking and drinking wine. Yesterday I was feeling a bit heavy and I got rid of my sadness by browsing in old bookshops and listening to light operas. I practice intensely the advice I give my students: follow music with the score to try to enter the mystery of the relationship between image and sound. (*7 September*)

***

I was filming objects (the tins I bought yesterday) with CNN TV in the background. Like apparitions. Actually, it's the only way I feel at ease filming: alone within four walls. It's about making those images, which inhabited houses of other times and that I saw while a typhus or tuberculosis happened, while the radio was broadcasting plays, confess their intimate secret. (*10 September*)

***

The passion, the vice for old books, like everything that touches men, is a confluence and dispersion of many currents, tendencies and cycles: 1) The cult of Ancestors (Gracián calls the act of reading «talking to the dead»). 2) Superior greed, such as numismatics and philately. 3) Stationary travel: touching a book that has passed through many hands. 4) Exploration (search for what has not been read by anyone). (Yesterday, in *El País*, talking about psychedelicism, they argued that drugs are a form of escape from what has already been seen, said, lived). 5) Recap: never the same book. 6) Response to the derealisation of the object, a book that can be touched and smelt (and this is the only way I can explain why I bought this notebook with paper full of signs that wants to be folded like a palimpsest). There are other reasons that can be applied to all collections: the creation of «paramarkets», the need to waste money, etc. (*10 September*)

***

Yesterday was a black day. Anniversary of the coup in Chile in 1973 and Tuesday like this day. Economic crisis, moral crisis. The USA are at war, but they do not know with whom or why. The diabolisation of America, which Che wanted, has been achieved by Islam. All signs of American power (and not only Wall Street money and the Pentagon) have entered a period of questioning (way of life, moral and political values). I should be happy but I am deeply saddened. I am reminded of Proust's idea that every extreme innovation brings about the resurrection of values that were thought to be dead and buried: the telephone and radio gave power to illiterate peasants and delusional fanatics. Magnetic tapes were instrumental in the seizing of power in Iran. The internet spreads overwhelmingly terrifying ideas and superstitions. (*12 September*)

***

I've spent a good part of the morning wandering around the house, especially in the library. Getting ready to attack the script I have to hand in before I leave. In fact, I've just realised that's what I want: to attack the script. I read a few pages of Carlo Ginzburg, then Renan's *Marc-Aurèle* and Proust's *The Guermantes Way*, Theodore Redpath's *Wittgenstein, A student's Memoir*, a couple of sonnets by Rustico Filippi, Sandra Laugier's *Wittgenstein*, a story from F. S. Fitzgerald's *Tales of the Jazz Age*. I wander somewhat chaotically, but not unpleasantly, while listening to Berg's String Quartet. Outside the sun appears and hides as soon as it senses my mood swings. Unless it's the opposite. I still don't know what to make for lunch. (*17 September*)

***

Reading, when I can, Carlo Ginzburg. It is strange how his preoccupations are the same as mine: Warburg, witchcraft, religious simulation (nicodemism), law and history. I guess one of these days I shall find him commenting on the topics of witchcraft and string theory. I would say that the preoccupations that keep me awake are of an Italian nature: Santillana, Storoni, Mazzolani, Agamben, Cacciari, Sciascia, Ginzburg, Macchia and, of course, Praz (let's not forget Elémire Zolla and Christina Campo). (*12 October*)

***

This morning I finished reading *A Closed Book*. Brilliant till the last fifteen pages, then an end a little sentimental that reminds me a bit of the Poirot TV series. Summary: a well-known writer, blind and cloistered in a castle or mansion, looks for an assistant. A young man arrives and takes up the position. Gradually the master-slave relationship changes into a duel: what the blind man remembers and continues seeing is subtly modified by the 'servant' until the house is transformed into a labyrinth. But in the end, we suddenly understand that the reason behind his behaviour is that when he was a child, he was raped by the old writer, and he's seeking revenge. He kills him, he is discovered, etc., which is a shame.

A 11 a.m. I have a meeting with Gilbert [Adair], and I'm thinking of proposing the following solution: the young man comes to take revenge, but gradually he lets himself become subjugated, seduced. In a certain way, he is raped again. The writer ends up killing him "in self-defence". He doesn't have any problem with justice, but the editor has the manuscript of the story that the young man, the victim, has written on what happened to him. The editor will publish it, it's called *I think you are in a nightmare*. The reaction of the writer is to kill himself in the same way the victim intended to kill him. We could film the two versions. One extra day. (*10 November*)

***

Taking up the idea put forward by Carlo Ginzburg (taken from a Russian structuralist I forget, a friend of Bakhtin's) [in *Wooden Eyes, Nine reflections on distance*]. It goes something like this: man, in the way he lives, is filled with vital automatisms that are of cultural, existential origin. (*12 December*)

***

Yesterday I talked about two issues with Patricio Rojas: a) In cinema, is it possible to talk about levels of reading? (I personally think not). b) Can we say that cinema, like art, is at the antipodes of literature (in the sense that literature is the art of making a blind person see while cinema is the art of blinding the sighted)?

Regarding the first issue, the flow of images and sounds in movement (and *of* movement) cannot be paused to be analysed. Therefore the flow turns into a swamp. There's a way, maybe a single one, of talking about cinema, that consists in dressing it with a flow of words (Joyce-like). That's to say, to swim in the river-film.

Regarding the second, what is blinding the sighted if not forcing him to re-examine the automatisms of vision that, without reflecting, we apply to a film as to reality? To give time to reflect. As much as the editing is accelerated, it can't escape the inertia of the centripetal function (which is as strong as the centrifugal vision that predominates in contemporary films). (*14 December*)

2002

*I*n Chez Gerald, opposite Avenida Perú (Viña del Mar), proletarianized, reading Max Scheler's *Metaphysics and the theory of culture*. On page 85 one finds his famous definition of "culture": "A well-read person is not someone who possesses knowledge and is familiar with *many* contingent modalities of things (*polimatía*), nor someone who can predict and command, in accordance with the laws, a maximum of events, but someone who possesses a personal structure, a combination of ideal movable schemes that, leaning on one another, construct the unity of a style and are used for intuitive knowledge, for thinking, conceiving, valorising the world and handling it". (*17 January*)

***

Starting this notebook on a cloudy January day, at lunchtime. Preparing a few films and finishing others. Tomorrow I leave for Rotterdam. As always, I carry on with the habit of writing in different notebooks the major and minor events of every day. Hearing and listening to Glenn Gould's *The well-tempered clavier*. (*24 January, PD*)

***

After a never-ending journey, I arrived just in time to take part in a debate on the end of cinema. We talked for an hour and a half. Everyone skirted around the problem without anyone daring to tackle what seems to me to be the main problem: apathy. The fact that ultimately everything is possible and that no one feels up to anything. (*25 January, PD*)

***

Rainy day. In a café on the Place Saint-Michel, reading *Troubadours et Trouvères* again, which I bought in Viña del Mar, in Librairie Altazor. Later I discovered that I knew the author, René Nelli, whose book *Du jeu subtil à l'amour fou*[21] I read years ago. Three days ago I bought his anthology of Occitan poetry. As I see it, I'm gradually getting into the troubadour poetry, I guess as the consequence of my intermittent keeping company with Chilean folksingers. (*28 January*)

***

Reading, or rather re-reading, Elémire Zolla's *The Invisible Mistress*, I came up with an idea for *Cagliostro:* it is a ghostly woman who reveals her powers and abilities to Balsamo. She will guide and teach him in dreams. She lives inside a diamond. That diamond will be stolen and taken away. And Cagliostro will pursue it until it reaches France, where it is hidden among other diamonds in the queen's necklace. Multiplication of diamonds. The diamond city in the centre of Africa, where all the «mother diamonds» come from, which communicate with each other and transmit «pyramidal clarity». (*31 January*)

***

I had an extensive dream, somewhat confusing. I had a ship at my disposal, but I realised that, at 60, I was no longer at the proper age to be the captain of the ship. I was preparing breakfast and broke a cup (last night I broke a champagne flute) and I was trying to hide the fact from the officer who was there to keep an eye on me or help me. In the end I decided to confess and even to accuse myself and this simple confession resulted in the broken cup mysteriously reassembling itself under our eyes. Then my father arrived and announced to my mother that he was inviting her to a restaurant that same night because the following day he had to leave for London. That minimal way of evoking a whole part of my life made me feel liberated and even happy when I woke up.

53

---

[21] Probably refers to the book *Raimon de Miraval. Du jeu subtil à l'amour fou*, texts and translations by René Nelli (Verdier, 1979).

I remember *Vidas Mínimas*, that book by González Vera. There are only minor lives, I should have said. (*2 February, PD*)

***

I found Francis Carco's *L'homme traqué* (ed. 1929) at a good price and considered, but did not buy, a 1790 edition of Molière, a first edition of Montesquieu's *Persian Letters*, a first edition of Pierre Loti's *Matelot* and the Lausanne edition (1748) of Rousseau's *Emile, or On Education*. Then I had lunch with the Rojas. Meanwhile I found time to read one of the strangest texts I have ever read, Suhrawardi's *Western Exile* (11th century), annotated by Abdelwahab Meddeb. It is a small text that has, at first reading, the form of a tale from *The Thousand and One Nights*, but with allegorical expressions that give the impression of dreaming while reading it. For example: «The city of men who cannot forgive», «The region of the central tree». I will come back to this text, which has awakened so many vocations and vacations. (*4 February, PD*)

***

I also read *Hoffmannia*, a script by Tarkovsky, extraordinary in that it combines the Slav spirit with German romanticism, I don't know how. I had the feeling of reading two texts superimposed. But isn't it the characteristic of cinema to create texts that work like palimpsests in motion? (*4 February, PD*)

***

Last night, dinner with Gérard Vincent. We talked about the troubadours. He's a real scholar. His thesis is that the troubadours formed a politico-poetic movement whose objective was to radically separate poetry from prose. In what way such a venture could be political is something I didn't quite understand, but Gérard seems to have good reasons to think so. I learned many things and above all, it gave me the incentive to delve a little more into that movement, which seems to turn its back on the problems of the century. The map of the troubadours is similar to that of the Cathar region. We know that they took part in Cathar ceremonies and that they adhered to that religion, but in their poems, little if nothing refers to the dualism. (*6 February, DP*)

***

I read a poem somewhat African by Desnos, and a chapter of Marguerite Yourcenar's *Fires*. This afternoon I have to finish the last scenes of *Un livre à rendre*. Then I shall carry on in parallel with *Cagliostro* and the preparation for my class, on Monday, in la Femis (a whole morning, which I see coming like a nightmare after a curanto[22]). I don't like today's young people, especially the French. I don't like people who want to be beautiful, rich and famous. But lately I've been experiencing an enthusiasm that's a little extravagant, despite the fact that there's nothing concrete about my projects. (*8 February, PD*)

***

I've been writing the presentation of my documentary on los Coyas, in Chile. The main idea of the documentary is to work around cultural identities. The Pitt Rivers have no crafts, no songs or stories. They are mechanics. We can say of them that they still live in the Stone Age, but have been able to learn quicker than others, to drive and repair cars and lorries. The Coyas, simple Chilean villagers, have invented a culture that distinguishes them from the rest. In doing so, they parody the process of re-education of Hispanic villages. I carried on reading Vargas Llosa's *The perpetual orgy*, and I still think that it could make a good fiction film. A literary essay treated as if it was fiction. (*28 February, PD*).

***

Yesterday I spent an uneventful day, but full of wrong expectations. I went out for a walk on the quay and bought a couple of books: a beautiful edition of *Gaspard de la nuit* and an early edition of Balzac (*The Middle Classes*). This morning I went out to visit a couple of antiquarian bookshops and found an original edition of Giono and one of Philippe Soupault. Now I'm in a café, where I've come to read the newspaper. The life of an old-age pensioner, almost. (*6 March*)

***

At the Lucenaire cinema, having dinner while they project *City of pirates*, a viewing for some ten people, among them at least five

---

[22] A shellfish stew from Chiloé. (trans.

Latino-Americans. I watched the first five minutes and I recognised and experienced again the energy and the excess of those years. I also felt again the precariousness and rigidity resulting from the basic and cumbersome means we had at our disposal. Many images come to me suddenly: Pina Bausch and Ronald Kay, my parents, Waldo and Ely and many others eating in Venice after the projection in the Festival's Official Selection, and without having money to pay for the dinner because Mitterand had forbidden the use of credit cards outside France. We only had hard cash (while in the bank, we had enough to celebrate for weeks). Today, I see again those images of another world, and I don't know what to think. The enormous energy from everyone, resulting in strong images. An unsophisticated, childish text, somewhat pedantic. But in the end, that's done. Life continues and the images stay, but I'm not sure it's a good thing. There is a lot of violence and intensity in the images, but also much pro-Third-World pedantry. Well, don't ask for pears from the apple tree. (*12 March*)

***

Yesterday, after three days of intensive labour, I watched in one go the four episodes (I should call them "cantos") of *Cofralandes*. Let's say that the "cantos" effect is starting to work. The five hours and more the edited material lasts, doesn't tire, oddly enough, it has the effect of *jogging*, or of a drug. One enters the game and is transported by a sort of inebriation that doesn't wear out but rouses. It is full of problems of various types, but nothing dramatic. The only thing is that I realised I am only at the beginning of my work. (*15 March, PD*)

***

In the afternoon I went to the left side of the river ("rive gauche", they call it) to look for some books I've had my eyes on for a month now. There was a second edition of *Double Heart* by M. Schowb with a dedication. I found a first edition of Francis Jammes with a dedication for 20 euros and a first edition of Lewis Carroll's *The Hunting of the Snark* for much more, but cheap given the usual price. I bought a second edition of *Les Amours jaunes* by Corbière. Good catch. Tonight we have a family dinner. It's nice to learn that in the bookshop I go to, I am the youngest customer (the average is 70). Tomorrow we'd have dinner with the Bouquins and the day after with the Prieurs. (*7 May*)

***

Yesterday I wrote no more than six pages. I read Schwob's *Double Heart* and a curious story by Ph. K. Dick in which two agents make a city disappear from Mars by putting it in a suitcase and taking it back to Earth. Reading an issue of an original magazine devoted to another magazine, *Le Grand Jeu,* in which there is an article on Jules Romains' experiences of extraretinal vision. Daumal let himself be the subject of these experiments, which consisted of placing an opaque glass box containing various objects – cards, figures, texts – illuminated by a light bulb. The subject was blindfolded and, at a certain time, the light bulb in the box, which was placed on the subject's chest, whose torso was naked, would be switched on, enabling him to see through the skin. The theory that Jules Romains wanted to prove was that there are cells in the skin that can transmit visual perceptions directly to the brain and that in the past men had a double vision system – through the eyes and through the skin – which allowed them, for example, to see in the dark (in caves?). (*11 May*)

***

I've read a book by Jacques Aumont, *Les théories des cinéastes.* It presents the most important theorisations of various directors and, at some point, comments on my theoretical approaches in *Poetics of cinema.* I have the feeling that he understood the propositions but not their consequences. (*14 May*)

***

Seen [Amos] Gitaï's film [*Kedma*][23]. Impressive. Good physiology. The place and what took place and what has to take place and always the place. What is a sacred territory? Buried, exiled or locked up, and always terrified.
There is no territory without Messiahs. Utopia without tops. Theory without *theor*: travel, single file, theatre, theory. The Sertão will become the sea, the sea will become the Sertão. (*16 May, PD*)

[23] Ruiz saw this and other films mentioned later when he was on the jury at the Cannes Festival.

Last night we saw Guédiguian's film *Marie Jo et ses deux amours*. Composed from moments of daily life. An unsustainable situation (a woman loves two men with the same intensity) that takes place between daily life events and ends up tainting everyday life with its insidious abnormality. At times it calls to mind the daily life of a person dying of an illness, in which moments gain in intensity due to the imminence of the tragedy. Toxic luminosity of the Mediterranean. The passing of days weaved like a tapestry from which an atmosphere gradually rises. Or several. *Climats*, André Maurois would say. A good balance of accents, a permanent problem with films from the south. Strangely enough, the character with the stronger accent is the most cosmopolitan. Jules and Jim revisited. With new intensity and uncertainty. Shot at an angle. Surprising (although not so much), the public's approval. Insidious landscape. Insistence on the prominence of the duration over the time of the play (the two hours of the film). Surprising the view from a window of the city while the day rises (image by image). Some criticisms: when the uneventful moments take place, one is gradually hostage to a tendency to "sampling", to typology. And because of the supremacy of the atmosphere, the scenes end up being interchangeable. A special mention for the use of nudity. It des-eroticises, makes them human: the discussion between Marie Jo and her lover in which, absorbed in the discussion, she forgets that she's naked. Surprising when one thinks that the script readers used to object to the excessive use of nudity. (*17 May, PD*)

Ken Loach's *Sweet Sixteen*. Free Cinema is back: the same indignation very well combined with a poetic atmosphere like the first films of T. Richardson, Karel Reisz and... Ken Loach. The carnality of the world of the [–], daily life in a nightmarish world and the almost intrusive presence of the landscape: the river, nature. The almost imperceptible transition from rebellious childhood to the business of crime. Ongoing poetry. (*21 May, PD*)

***

Yesterday we had the second meeting of the jury and I had a few interactions with the rest of the jury. But today, I had my first deep *shock*: Sokurov's film [*Russian Ark*] is a milestone in the history of cinema. (*22 May, PD*)

***

The scenography for *Medea* is made of three screens, vertical projections in which anamorphic images appear in the manner of El Greco. The basic idea is that of Florensky in *Reverse Perspective*. At least an aspect of it: the distant objects and characters are bigger than those nearest. (*5 June*)

***

Yesterday I was reading Nabokov's *Ada*, in which the possibility of thinking by means of a visual series of algorithms is discussed. Tomorrow I start preparing the filming of the projected backgrounds for the opera *Medea*. (*30 June, PD*)

***

Two nights ago, during an hour and a half of insomnia (between 4 and 5.30 a.m.) I distracted myself imagining new narrative modes. For example, one hands out to the assistant a perfectly coherent script that tells a story and solves it. The assistant has the working plan. He decides to start in the middle, then wanderings through the streets would follow, then to set 8, let's say that the story starts and ends in set 8, etc. Once the working plan done, one considers that this plan *is* the film and the latter is edited according to that order. What type of film would that method give? (*10 July, PD*)

***

I carried on thinking about the Orphic gold tablets as ceremony and metaphor for cinema. I summarise: When we die we forget everything, but there is a gold tablet next to our body. It is an *aide-mémoire*. On it is written that the soul expects to find a spring near a cypress but that it must avoid it in spite of being thirsty. Further away it will find a stream or a river watched by guards. It must pass a questioning of sort and finally will be able to drink the water of the river that comes from the lake of

59

Mnemosyne and that way, it will recover its memory. But what memory? Is it the memory of things from one's personal life? Maybe it is an archetypical memory. The memory that a film should awaken in us. Recollections of icons made of intensities never experienced but sensed. Recollection or nostalgia for an iconostasis shared and yet intimately connected to each one. (*29 August, PD*)[24]

***

Gradually I think of ideas for a film that I've had in mind for twenty years. My first idea was to film, in parallel, the processes of Góngora's purity of blood and Tasso's *Amintas*. Then, years later, I became interested in the case of the inquisitor Carranza and recently, something around the defence of Austria. Behind everything stands the figure of a delusional and formalist Spain as shown by Ortega. (*1 September, PD*)

***

Last night I went to see a film [*Tres noches y un sábado*] by [Joaquín] Eyzaguirre, that entertained me at times, intrigued me. A lot of material a little bit too much, piling up. The audience was delighted. It's obvious that Chilean cinema has specialised in comedies. We had planned to talk after dinner, but it didn't happen. The original sin of all Chilean and part of Latin American cinema is the lack of a dynamic principle in the staging. (*2 September, DP*)

***

Four days in San Sebastían are enough, seeing friends and a few (actually nothing) films. Yesterday the six hours of *Cofralandes* were shown and seen by very few people. In the last episode, which is the one I like the most, there was no one there. Then we went for lunch with our friends from Guetaria. These last few days we have eaten, drunk and strolled. We have to face up to the fact that my films are of no interest at all. The only people who were curious, apart from our friends, were French. I've tried to read a little, but the over-indulgence has dulled my brain. This morning I went to a bookshop and bought a second edition of Ortega's *Invertebrate Spain* (from the same year as the first). (*24 September*)

[24] Echoing a previous reading, recorded on 7 July: "I read a book somewhat academic by Giovanni Pugliese dedicated to the study of the Orphic gold plates. Small messages destined for the afterlife. They are admonitions to the deceased."

I went to Radio France for an interview, a meeting with Boris Cyrulnik. We talked about the function of art, a subject that Cyrulnik introduced. According to him, without fiction and images, people would live in a permanent present. I expounded on Ulam's idea of visual language and he told me that thanks to people like Ulam (he quoted two others) ethologists could now investigate the non-language thinking of children under the age of 3, as some ten years ago, no one paid attention to children's thinking until they began to speak. And before the age of 3, human beings are intensely intellectually and emotionally active. All of a sudden I began to think that the paradise we have lost was experienced in early childhood and that we were banished from it by language and then lived in exile in the land of formalised logos, which is the language from which we sometimes try to escape with the help of poetry. (There is poetry when language goes on vacation, according to Wittgenstein). (*26 September*)

***

I finish reading Truman Capote's *Shut a final door*. I read it around 40 years ago, and I don't think I've read it since. I experience the same emotion. Confusion, anxiety and a very particular sadness. I realise that *That day* owes a lot to that small pale-blond. One objection: much of the disquietude comes from the homosexual background and if it becomes too explicit, the story weakens, but it is only my take on it. It gives me back my desire to live. (*1 October, PD*)

***

Reading Nerval [*Aurelia*]. *Shock*. I had never read the insane between the lines. The clairvoyant insanity had never seemed so clear to me. (*7 October*)

***

Can we talk of re-reading? In reality, a text, despite its apparent lightness, has a plurality of connections that give it the look of tissues in the body (in the manner of *falls* – Freud – in sleep), like concretions that give at each reading a new hierarchy to the texts read and therefore a modification on the periphery, which results in a new reading each time, depending of course on the richness of the text. (*6 October*)

***

It's strange writing in different diaries at the same time [for the moment there are three, but soon there will be four or five]. It creates the illusion of a plot between my various identities. I feel like a multinational competing with itself. (*27 October*)

***

Today, looking around my library, I came across a book of analytical philosophy [Nagel] whose title made me want to write an essay: *The viewpoint from nowhere*. In the terminology of frames in the USA, apparently the names of camera angles have been exhausted: viewpoint from A or B, etc. Viewpoint of someone, *limbo shots*, etc. But what about the viewpoint of the viewpoint? Someone looks at something from a window. We see what is seen but, with a little ingenuity, we can also show "the fact of looking through the window". Cinema watching itself watching. (*20 November*)

***

Last night, I mentally edited the film [*Strong Souls*] again, and I'm already seeing it. Yet the most complex is that the synthesis that is produced at the moment of filming has an intense rhythm, which means that the six functions overlap in such a way that there is tension between them. The moment when various shots fuse into a single one has an *oneiric* content, namely, one dreams. As in dreams, there is a shift of the normal components, in such a way that each gesture gives the impression of happening in a *mental universe*. "night of iron morning of ice / cry encircled by the flame of silence / and you right in the middle of the open fruit of the day / what are you waiting for where are you going lost root / I await the first moss and the cry of the lamb / the secret bee the axe in the forest / an imperceptible step of mist and milk / a hollow saw in the confines of summer" (Tristan Tzara). (*20 November*)

***

In the taxi this morning, coming to the Flore, an uchronia came to mind: according to a truism transmitted through generations, if South America had been conquered by the English, today it wouldn't be much different from the USA. But what if it was more like India? Namely a continent in which the great ancient civilisations, the Incas, the Aztecs would dominate and with the intervention of England, would have occupied the rest of America. The natives would have kept their customs: dress, language, religion. History could be told like a soap opera: small scenes in which the general situation will gradually appear, without it suggesting a grand spectacle (as happens in Kramer's first socio-fictions). (*23 November*)

***

Gathering ideas for the uchronic film. First scene: a Nahuatl scholar translates *Time Regained* into Nahuatl. The text has given him asthma and he gradually dies. Before he dies he is visited by Proust. 1) 1920. 2) A bookshop, a collector is looking for an uchronia. History of Spain: he imagines that Spain conquered America. 1970. 3) An encounter in London: a Mapuche Christian guerrilla fighter resisting invaders who want to impose their religion. 4) Etc. In the end a kaleidoscopic theory of time (that is, cinema). (*24 November*)

***

In front of Lake Geneva. In the morning we filmed the journey of Treffle and Warff[25] in the hills. Last night I finished reading *The Inquiry*. Somewhat disappointed with the ending. The riddle is not solved. It opens up options, but doesn't close any of them. Tomorrow Valeria arrives. Perplexity about the future. I don't really know which film to make. Health faltering. Lausanne sad. Film sad. But good mood in the team. Amazing silence. In an hour we return to Lausanne. I count on a few pages of Whitehead to revive me. The hotel, frankly disconcerting. Chile far away. So much the better. Cold, benevolent air. Death circling. Death circular. (*27 November*)

***

[*Medea*]. Tomorrow I shall go and get *The origins of tragedy*, which must be one of the books that I don't have yet. The basic elements are in the texts that I wrote years ago in "Por un teatro astronómico". Other books that come to mind: Aby Warburg's *Essais florentins*, Ruffini's *Fiestas del Renacimiento*, *Hamlet's Mill* by Santillana, the prologue to the stories of Kordofán by Frobenius. (*4 December*)

63

---

[25] Characters in *That day* (2003).

***

I've been thinking about that expression that came to me years ago in front of Javier Ruiz and which made him take a leap forward: «More than a reader, I'm a book diviner». A book diviner. But I can also say that I am a diviner of lives: don't I have the impression of having lived no lives and divined many? Or should I say "glimpsed at", «sighted»? I sight them, but do they sight me? I say this in connection with *Medea*, the novel by Christa Wolf. I had it in front of me several times, leafed through it, read a total of about twenty pages and divined at several possible novels. As I will have read it in a couple of days' time, it is possible that these possible novels will expand the actual text. In that case, reading, if practiced in that way, systematically, would always be a rereading. (*10 December*)

***

At the station I bought a book by Claude Michel Cluny, about whom I knew nothing. He is a much-appreciated poet whose diaries, the first dating between 1948 and 1960, are gradually being published [he was born in 1930]. He won the Renaudot Prize. I'm reading it in parallel with the Goncourt Prize [Quignard] and both books merge in a strange way: one is searching for a novel, the other for an essay, and both are diaries. Like my own, and, apart from the desire, on the part of those two, to make literature not very far from my own. A week ago, all of a sudden, Valeria asked me: "Why make a personal diary? To read it again? To publish it?" Deep down, she's asking: Why write? And, further than that, why culture, why memory? The question is not stupid, but impossible to answer. The relation between question and answer is not far from the relation between a text in one language and its translation. To translate is to answer, to answer is to think, to think is to answer assertions prior to the question. (*22 December*)

***

[*Medea*]. A few notes to communicate to the extras tomorrow. What is an extra? In most theatre plays or musicals, the extra fulfils at least three functions: a) The witness is the crowd that follows or generates the peripetia. b) They are a prolongation of the set, they are used to modify it. In Italy it is the servant in the scene, in Spain, the scene-shifter. c) They are the mediator between what is outside the scene and what we see, and between the set and the actors. In our case, those three functions are combined in the following manner: the set is movable and motionless, it is active and passive. In order for the movements to integrate the action, the mediators are necessary: sometimes they are the witnesses of the scenery and turn their backs to the staging, sometimes they are secretions of the scenery. But there is more: they can transmit the drowsiness or the statism of the scenery to the scene. They can comment and criticise the scene. (*22 December*)

***

Last night I had dinner at Guyon's house with his wife and their two children, a young man studying Fine Arts and his 15 years old sister who wants to be a film maker. The parents wanted me to speak about the difficulties and the agonies of cinema, but I could not. Cinema must be the most enjoyable profession that exists. (*24 December*)

***

[Medea]. The show is what it is: a contemporary opera treated as [Alban] Berg recommends, "the old-fashioned way". (*24 December*)

***

This morning I was thinking about a new project, *Olvidos*: an old professor gradually gets lost in a labyrinth of minute forgetfulness as he writes a treatise on hope and randomly meets different characters who all personify the angel of death; he tries to convince his son, on holiday in Chile, not to commit suicide, while the idea of death gradually takes over his life. I don't know what can be made of such a melancholic subject, but I do know that it's a good project to make in digital video. (*26 December*)

***

Moments of indecision this morning in front of a bookcase, not knowing what book to take. In the end I read the study on *Armance*. A good idea. Stendhal had decided to not explain the impotence of his protagonist, not out of decency, but for the sake of the secret.

What is the function of the secret in a film? On the condition of working a closed narrative system. Scholem: the secret dimension of language. The mystic discovers in language something that relates to its structure and is not suited to communicate what is transmissible except – and all symbolism is based on that paradox – in communicating what is *not transmissible*, what exists in it and whose expression it is not. (*29 December*)

***

I remember a Chilean (or other) joke that gives an idea of an aspect of the cabal, of trickery. Someone says: «There is an animal that clucks, has feathers, lays eggs that are edible and has three legs.» And the other: «I don't know.» The first: "A hen." «But the hen has two legs.» «Yes, but if I told you, you would have guessed easily (straightaway).» The end. Can such a trick have an aesthetic function? If we understand that an aesthetic function leads to emotions of the type: exultant perplexity, rapture, vertigo, exhilaration, etc. (but what is this «etc.»?). Memento: the Monte Carlo Method makes it possible to cover, go through and synthesise extremely complex mathematical processes. In cinema, what does it mean to use a trap? Let's imagine a shot/reverse-shot in which we have settled comfortably and in which suddenly a character we don't know appears, who answers to one of the two interlocutors of the shot/reverse-shot, and before we have time to realise it, the interlocutor to whom we had become accustomed, reappears. Someone will say on seeing it: «It's a useful image» (but of which of the two characters?). Another: «It's a flashback» (but of what?). Another: «It's a ghost». Very few will say: «It's a trick», but it is certain that the disturbance will provoke greater intensity in the viewer's attention. They will want to see the scene again, to claim that they saw what they saw. Solecisms work in another way. In *Medea* the break-up scene between Jason and Medea is done as a love scene, and the contradiction accentuates its meaning. (*29 December*)

2003

*I*t seems that the costs of the elements of digital productions continue to fall and we can expect, without being pessimistic, that soon entire layouts will be requested before making a film. The polarisation of the productions has already taken place. The erosion of the technical aspect too. Marxism is coming back. A neo-Marxism that analyses the fetishisation of the world and games as motor of production.

"I looked back and I saw that the most agile don't always win the race, nor the strongest win the fight, nor the most intelligent or the wisest govern, because all are subjected to time and chance."

"Religion is what man does with his solitude." (Whitehead, *Religion in the making*)

Cinema is the art of creating systems from unique and incomparable events (by opposition to music). Another: cinema is elements united by poetry (in the sense of creative madness). (*6 January*)

***

Herbart's novel *[La Licorne]* seems to have been written for me. It contains all the elements that I like: ambiguity of emotions, labyrinthine space, oddness: a house without bedrooms in which, without planning it, the residents have decided to never sleep in the same place and move from one place to another like sleepwalkers, without schedule, without time. Atmosphere of incest. Absence of the outside world. Etc. (*6 January*)

***

An idea that I'm interested to connect with the ambiguity of feelings: the ambiguity of space. To create a modular house made of different houses, at times isolated, at times with a view on a beach, very crowded, or in the suburbs of a big city. The periods also change. It's possible that those holidays lasted many years. (*7 January*)

***

Quiet night. Pain in my kidney. Normal glycemia. Rapid pulse. Slight tremor of the hands. Permanent lumbago. Weakness of the legs and above all a lot of sadness. If the film *That day* had been killed in production, I could at least have complained or fought, but the way it was produced has condemned it to be stillborn. (*15 January*)

***

Agamben, in his essay called "The dream of language", on *Hypnero-tomachia Poliphili*, maintains that Francesco Colonna's intention, project, plan or plot was to shape a monster in which the words were Italian, common, and the structure, Greco-Latin. And he associates this project with Mallarmé's idea of giving a specific weight to each word by isolating it from the sentence. I would say that my project is to disassemble the film so that each frame has its own life. It remains to be done. (*18 January*)

***

Yesterday, explaining my way of working to Valérie Kaprisky, I realised some weaknesses, or, rather, that the method has its advantages but lacks development. In the coming days, I will see if I can develop some of its aspects. In principle (if there is one) it would be that a character should never be constructed in isolation but in relation to those others, close to it. Another principle is that one must separate *structure* from *construction*. The structure is volitional, it's given once, it is the skeleton. The construction is the ensemble of behaviours that escape the structure. The ensemble of acts and automatic or unconscious opinions. The distinction structure-construction is Florenski's. (*5 February*)

***

Going back on *structure* and *construction,* both are contaminated by the notion of *paradigm*: "The set of unconscious opinions on a theme" (Kuhn). What is the industrial narrative paradigm? In short, it is the set of narrative impulses that guide a unique story. A narrative impulse is the irresistible tendency to complete a *narrative syllogism* instantly. A narrative syllogism is the smallest narrative unity that tends to be linked to a story – always the same – structured like the central conflict. Example: *An honest man lives five minutes of dishonesty. A dishonest man lives five minutes of honesty. And both change their lives.* When a minimum of reason would bring us to say: "it depends on which honest or dishonest gesture", or more simply, "nothing much will happen". (*5 February*)

***

In a certain way, for us quantum physics implies a kind of anti-memory with recollections of the future, many futures that stabilise with the particles of the past, of the multiple pasts. As a matter of fact, many things that I have lived, in reality I have dreamed them, or, more still, I have glimpsed them in dreams. Analogies between the loops of the particles and the "non-place" of certain dreams. How many phenomena does the word dream include? How many convergent or divergent processes? (*8 February*)

***

When I was mentally editing the film, I had doubts about the hand-held camera sequence. Perhaps the hand-held camera shots should be complemented by general shots seen from above. Finally, the principle of staging is that what we see is being seen permanently by two ghosts. That is to say that the mapping function predominates (things seen from above and far away). *Revising several notions*: The combinatory function posits that what we are seeing is one of the possible editings. Which is one way to integrate a situation that is more accentuated every day, meaning that the film is one of the possibilities of the matrix of the film. *Note for an essay*: Cinema as amnesia. What we are seeing we have already seen it but we have forgotten it. For that, to play with the idea of "déja vu". To arrange framing, voices, echoes. (*26 February*)

***

Yesterday, I had dinner with the consul for Chile, who turned out to be a philosopher, a specialist in Heidegger. The woman director of the Cervantes Institute and the commercial (and cultural) attaché for

Mexico also came. We said many things but nothing about cinema. Like most Spanish-speaking intellectuals, they think that cinema is an activity presenting no interest and used solely to earn money and celebrity by entertaining simple folks. Having fled Latin America, the continent of desire and sadness, is one of the few things I don't regret. (*dixit* Keyserling). (*1 March*)

***

Disagreeable feeling of being famous, which intensified with the reading of a book of interviews with Dürrenmatt that I read yesterday and which in many aspects seems the book that accompanies my retrospective in Bobigny[26]: evocation of childhood (fake and mythologised), ideas on this and that and everything in general. The sensation of being buried alive. (*16 March*)

***

In the plane. Chileans on all sides. More Chileans than Argentines. From the start the plane was full. The self-satisfied and cynical smile of my compatriots. The same sensation each time I go to Chile: That was a close call! The same impression that they are not all murderers, but that they would get pleasure from killing me. I brought Jean Lévi's *La Mission*, *Orlac's Hands* and Carlo Ginzburg's *Wooden Eyes*, to read on the plane. That should be enough. No newspapers or magazines. Next to me a reader of *Le Figaro*. (*8 April*)

***

Hard day: feeling sick, feverish and… much work to do. We kept to the plan but I'm still feeling ill. This morning I finished working on the *Mara Schwartz* saga, twelve pages. I think it's good and no one can say I did it for money. Paulo calls again, enthusiastic. *That day* still works. And I still don't like it. Tomorrow morning I have to have some tests. I'm beginning to capitulate unconditionally. Some of the prospects: Parkinson's, dialysis, amputations, blindness. All in ten years' time. Life is short. Wine is generous, and the French? I don't know. It would be worse in Chile. (*10 June*)

***

Bakhtin: "The role of art is to fight the automatisms created by the gestures and acts of survival". Brice Parain in a Godard film: Athos (one

[26] It refers to Théâtres au cinéma, n° 14: Raoul Ruiz. Published for the 14th festival of Bobigny, 11-28 March 2003.

of The Three Musketeers) escapes from a house on fire, and all of a sudden wonders if it's possible for someone to put one foot in front of the other so quickly when running. The thought stops him in his tracks and he dies. Physical and mental automatism. In cinema (in any audiovisual flow) one believes that one image comes after another. Including in *zapping*. Let's imagine that the image is not followed by an image (that we don't see because we have changed channel), etc. And that B is followed by an image C, that we don't see either because we have changed channel again. In fact, each new image involves a change of channel. In a film of 500 frames, there are 500 changes of channel. Which means, we have seen 500 fragments of film. Let's imagine that each fragment is autonomous: we have seen 500 films. Let's go back to the metaphor of *zapping*. Each frame involves a change of channel, but we only have at our disposal ten channels. Each change of channel shows us an image between one and ten. Each ten changes we go back to see a second fragment of the film. After a while, we start to recognise the films. We prefer the fourth and the seventh. After a certain time we move exclusively between the fourth and the seventh. Of course from time to time, following what is called "the Martinoya cycles", we peep at other films to see if we still don't like them. We can follow indefinitely that conceptual simulation. For the time being we can keep in mind that when we see a film, in reality we see many films. And that there are two ways of dealing with the problem: or we try to make the viewer forget the multiplicity of films or we try to keep it *always present*. Two grammars, two rhetorics, diametrically different, confront each other. I personally prefer a third solution. Initially accentuate the effect of continuity then gradually break it. (*15 June*)

***

Reflecting. Visions of the oceanic past and the narrow future. How many friends are peacefully moving closer to suicide? *No judgement!* Alone in an empty Indian restaurant. Life and death "interweaved". Silent sedition. *Fitna*[27]. Stealth, Caution. Namely, Spinoza. (*16 June*)

***

Lethal dinner with Benoît Peeters, Pierre Arditi, [François] Schuiten. Many bottles of Bordeaux consumed with excess in a short period of

71

---

[27] 'Affliction' in Arabic.

time. Confusing dreams and intense work. I started to read Laín Entralgo's *La Generación del 98*. Nothing new. Much reminiscence and something of a weary pain. Old age, moribund-ness. (*18 June*)

***

All morning conversing, discussing (little), they listen, I speak, I almost digress, but go back in an incantatory way on some themes: the combinatory, the independence of the frame, magic, the combination of rational and magic thought. Life is a dream, the recurrent theme of the 98 generation. Life hungry for dreams. "This life hungry for dreams". (*20 June*)

***

Writing with the Dunhill pen that Valeria gave me years ago and which I hadn't used for several months. I spent a perfectly idle day. In the morning I listened to *Les Mamelles de Tirésias* by Poulenc-Apollinaire. Then Emilio [Del Solar] arrived and we discussed philosophical problems for a couple of hours. We wrote a page of notes. I reread: is forgetting positive or negative? Negative forgetting: forgetting of forgetting. There are stages in the process of forgetting. Can forgetting be an emotion? In any case there are strong emotions that emerge from forgotten worlds. (*14 July*)

***

After a long siesta I read two chapters of *A perfect friend*. The story of a man in the middle of life's journey who, after receiving a blow, loses his memory. A very banal subject, except that the author apparently suffered a similar mishap and found himself in that strange world full of holes and shadow zones, of amnesiacs. A world that in the end is not very different from our own. We too are full of forgotten regions and days, and those days form years. Days here, days there, that form turbulent regions. Not the unconscious, where there is no forgetting, but anti-forgetting or counter-forgetting. «X became distracted from life until he forgot everything. Only then did he remember that he had forgotten to forget». He forgot everything except the act of forgetting. Is it an act? Dreaming is a form of forgetting. In the Chilean countryside for «awakening» they say «remembering», and Jorge Manrique: «Remember the sleeping soul», and so on.

Going back to the conversations with Emilio [Del Solar], what does the one who forgets forget? Skeleton of memories. Skeleton and scheme. Memory as duration. Music as memory and as forgetting. One can imagine «trans-memories» that feed on forgetting. The field, the territory of forgetting, is intertwined with that of remembering. (*15 July*)

***

Old age is arriving at top speed and almost catches me without weapons. And the weapons of old age are ruse and foresight. (*17July*)

***

Schiele: "Death in life". To live is to die. And to die is to live. To die a little. But what is this little? Given that life is holistic, a piece is also the whole. (*29 July*)

***

In the afternoon, I read the two first chapters of *Perspectives on General System Theory*, by Ludwig von Bertalanffy, who introduced the theory of open systems, used in medicine and biology. There's an aspect that enables its application to cinema; a system is open when the exchange with the outside world is intense to the point of involving all its components (a human body renews itself in parts permanently, and in total, every 6 months). The majority of works of art are closed and incomplete systems that necessitate a spectator as parasite in order to be complete. Cinema can function as an open system in the sense that it can integrate a real (or oneiric) audiovisual flow. To be revised. (*Sunday 3 August*)

***

Bertalanffy: Man doesn't live in a world of things, but in a world of symbols. The objectification of symbols is the cause of the malaise of our times: remove from the fabric of symbols all uniqueness. Make them interchangeable. (*3 August*)

73

***

As we know, American films allow for a decorative, therefore expressive, element, what they call *symbols*: allegoric particles that have for objective to give an emotional synthesis of the film. In *The Quiet American*, there is only one: at a certain point there is an attack and the person indirectly responsible, a CIA agent, tries in an ambiguous way to help and at the same time to distance himself from the events (the American foreign policy of those years). An American takes out his handkerchief and tries to wipe the blood that smears his shoes. The image has something of a visual solecism, that interested Klossowski so much: a symbol that by its ambiguity, accentuates the enigma. An anti-allegorical element, in this sense. (*25 August*)

***

[...] *Stalker*, by Tarkovsky. A lot to say about the coexistence of many films in a single one. The fantasy aspect and the premonitory images (the implosion of socialism). (*31 August*)

***

Act of divination: Javier Ruiz thinks he knows that José Lezama Lima was a «great diviner» of libraries. In the construction of a library, what path do we follow, what thread do we lose? More than a labyrinth, or a visual image, the library is a tapestry. A weaving of states of consciousness. For example, in my studio one can say that there are books of bibliographic value from the past, from the 16th, 17th, 18th, 19th and early 20th centuries. But there is also a second criterion. Books in English, German, Italian, Spanish and, at the same time, books banned by the Church, books about Jansenism and the enthusiasts (Rabaut, Dupuis, Boulanger). Valuable manuscripts and journals. However, *La Révolution surréaliste* is shelved next to some condemnations of the Inquisition and papers from the trial of Tupac Amaru and a manuscript book or notebook with recipes for cooking and medicines, in which one can find some Bonapartist songs. (*10 September*)

***

David Bohm's idea: in a fish tank a fish is filmed with two cameras and in an adjacent space the images are projected, so that the illusion is given that two different fish are being seen. Looking at the two images, we think we are watching two different fish, but in the fish tank we discover that there is only one fish. We can proceed in this way to unify sequences that appear to be different. The unification can be done in stages. We can also integrate time, so that sequences separated in time actually happen simultaneously: many characters are one at different times, which are reconstituted inversely. (*21 September*)

***

Rereading some passages of Agamben's *The end of the poem*. It's raining, and as Pezoa Véliz says, with rain, "anxiety falls". Sharp, intense feeling that I'm not going to return to Chile (false), strange recollections. "Vague disquietude". (*27 September*)

***

Yesterday, walking home, I bumped into a musician friend and collaborator of Benoît Peeters in the street. We had a coffee and talked a bit about the connections between the musical structure, the sonorous plot (not the same thing) and its connections with the visual plot (the shots) and the visual structure. It becomes increasingly clear to me that the sound and visual weaves should be inseparable and create a whole with the narrative weave. The relationship of the weaves would be implicit as opposed to the structural relationships, which would be explicit (although one might think otherwise: in fact what we see and hear are foreground relationships of images and sounds expelling micro-fictions that associate, but also conspire against the strategic fiction). The strategic fiction, the main story of the film, the explicit element (main discourse, rather decourse), is integrated into the overflowing discourse of the audiovisual micro-organisms. (*4 October*)

***

Noon. Reading Cassian's *Cenobitic Institutions*, the chapter on sadness, the fifth capital sin. I am discovering that sadness is not exactly boredom, which would be a mixture of sadness and laziness, which is indeed linked to the Demon of Noon. There is a good sadness and a bad sadness: the one that comes from the fact that we recognise our faults and we are sorry for having strayed from harmony (from God) and the «sadness of the age», which comes from having lost things of this world for they were «too good». And laziness is active, it is the uprootedness that causes the feeling of loosing something. (*19 October*)

***

In the evening, several images appeared to me – situations that go back and forth between my personal life and a film (*Un livre à rendre*) that I am preparing. More than ever, it seems clear to me that a film is a receptacle. In so far as it receives from the spectator, it begins to live until it becomes an active agent. It is the film that looks at the spectator. And one can even get to the point when the spectator looks sideways at the film that looks at him. Something similar to the furtive glances exchanged between two lovers who are looking for each other. (*1 November*)

***

In a bookshop I saw an old edition, a first printing, of Nodier's short stories. The Inquisition abounds in bookshops. The Inquisition rather than bad faith. It is difficult to agree on the notion of «original edition», «first edition», «first printing». The Inquisition starts in the publishing houses. In England it is worse because there are English first editions, but appearing later than the American or Australian. Slowly I've started to work on the reduction of *Klimt*'s script. It's 10.20 am. At 1 pm they're dropping off an order of wine. (*7 November*)

***

In the morning I read two stories by Nodier. In one of them he develops the strange theory (which he traces back to Pliny) according to which «dreams are transmitted». They are contagious either by neighbourliness (one communicates dreams to one's neighbour while sleeping), or by narration. Wittgenstein's test (dreams are a language only if they pass the test of double translation): I dream something, I tell it to someone and that someone in turn has the same dream as me. (*13 November*)

***

Notes for the speech[28] : 1) In the 60s, when I started, cinema was still mechanical. 2) Technicians have moved from the analogue shutter to the digital shutter and finally to the progressive shutter. 3) The role of the

[28] It refers to the speech he had to make for the "Master of Cinema" prize awarded to him by the Manheim-Heidelberg International Film Festival.

filmmaker has changed from total artist to a form of guerrilla warfare. (*21 November*)

***

Today I have seen the material that I need sent to Rotterdam. A few scenes from *Comedia de sombras* and notes of the Circle of Belleville and notes on *Poetics of cinema*. Gradually I'm creating a personal poetic system. (*30 November*)

***

At the Clown Bar, waiting for Gérard Vaugeois to examine the latest news about *Klimt*. Today I finished reading and reading again my old script of *The Man Who Was Thursday*. A real concentrate of English analytical philosophy. Seen from a distance it has something of a *Harry Potter* for grown-ups. There is poetic inspiration, it is funny. It lacks, I would say, human warmth. I must read Chesterton's original again. At this point it is difficult for me to distinguish what is Chesterton's and what I have invented (my chameleon side again). I read an interview of Bergier against Gurdjieff in the surrealist magazine *Medium*. Coming to the restaurant I walked past an amazing esoteric bookshop, where I bought a book about the Thule sect. All this must come from last night when I saw *The Great Dictator*. I had forgotten a good part of it. Ambiguous impression of the last speech. You'd think George Bush talking about Iraq. (*23 December*)

2004

*T*o recapitulate: in *Un livre à rendre,* the staging system is based on a set of mental images produced by the brain of a man in his 70s and something that has already begun to «ramble». What is a mental image? It's an everyday image with an eccentric, atrabilious element. A room with a chair, above it a window with daylight and a window with night light. Perhaps a sleeping crocodile might be useful. (*25 March*)

***

The distinction between implicit and explicit order can be applied to the structure of a film independently of the dissipative structure. Also the deductive (a structure put into images) and inductive construction of the general narrative model arises in particular from a connection between images. Of course, there are procedures that can be gradually clarified: structure from connections of two images. Concretions: several shots become one. Priorities. It is necessary to imagine in permanence the superimposition of several shots or, rather, several flows of images, so that submerged images can appear suddenly or gradually. Interrupted flows within an uninterrupted flow. Imagine a film flowing in several directions. (*25 March*)

***

On the plane, waiting to take-off for Madrid. Already a bit dizzy and faint. I read diaries, and thought about pictures. I have more or less read a book about Borges in the form of a manual that made him odious to me. Almost very odious, as inelegant as the expression is. A little recap: June: *Un livre à rendre*. October: *Klimt*. August: *Ethnicities*. December: *Ethnicities*. January: *A Closed Book*. March: *Ethnic Fictions*. May: *Orlac's Hands*. October: *La Mission.* A lot is a lot: one good six others remain. Filming for the sake of filming. All around me only Spanish accents. Horrible. (*4 May*)

***

Reading Stephen King. He managed to draw me into his story: a plane that loses half of its passengers. It makes me want to go back on my idea in the manner of Hoffmann's cat Murr. The text of a bestseller from the 1950s and opposite, a text that is the decoding of the first, until the functions are reversed, complicated, interwoven, and the whole is the sacred book of a sect. Taking literally Klossowski's idea of literature as plot. Also thinking of doing something with Paracelsus' treatises. (*13 May*)

***

I had a theoretical dream: any filmed scene has (can have) a holographic structure, which means it can break down into parts equivalent to the whole – the complete scene – but these parts are, let's say, «indiscernible», that is not delimitable. The totalities are constructed in overlapping narratives, of which each emerging segment is the visible part. Each scene is a flattened cube. It is worth what it is worth. First day of filming. (*31 May*)

***

Rainy day. Heavy night. Enthusiastic morning. New projects and suddenly a phone call and melancholy takes over. Trying to pull myself together. A cup of coffee. Trying again to get into the new projects: 1) *Ethnicities* (the three fictions). 2) *Ilinx* (back to Kafka). 3) *Vernissage* (a Hitler uchronia). 4) *Theor* (futuristic thriller about the implant of telephones in the brain and the disappearance of introspection and egocentric discourse). 5) *Lethal Sea* (?) and the others: *Orlac's Hands, Cagliostro, A Closed Book, Malpertuis*. Nine projects (two, three years?). At the moment I'd like to start working on the script for *Vernissage*. (*6 June*)

***

A problem close to dissipative structures arises in the construction of a film, specifically at the moment of «invention», that is to say, of its ultimate planning, just before filming. In fact, any script, even the most anarchic, tends to propose a mechanical filming. It tends towards balance. A film (and any work of art) being an unbalanced and dynamic form, let's say a vortex, any intrusion of forms leading to equilibrium kills it. [...] What do I mean when I say that each shot of a film is itself a film? This intuition can take us very far. For example, we can say that each shot is an open window to another universe or, better – the word «window» being open to misunderstanding – a continuum that escapes us and contains what's outside the film. The interferences in wave mechanics are a good image for a new way of understanding editing. (*22 June*)

***

This morning in a café I finished reading *Distant Star* and started *Monsieur Pain*, also by Bolaño. I don't know what to think. He has a good style and a wide imaginary world, but there's something resentful that marks him as provincial (the same applies to Muñoz Molina and almost all Chilean writers, but not in the same way to the Argentinians). (*25 August*)

***

I spoke with Valeria, she's just seen *Miss Dalloway* (sic), based on the novel by Virginia Wolf, and is convinced that the melancholic aspect of the film comes from the combination of various eras. But they are combinations of discreet moments, and not the fusion of times like I appreciate, in which all the periods, as in a polyhedron made of unique durations that by miracle link together, make us glimpse at multiple temporalities with a force that gives them life. (*5 September*)

***

Cinema: the art of playing with the irreversible. Goethe: poetry is not a science or an art, it is genius (inspiration). To master the irreversibility of actions with the magic of connections (Bruno). "It is necessary that those who must work on reality using connections possess, in a certain way, a universal theory of things, to be able to captivate men" (read: irreversible time). (*14 September*)

***

Arriving beforehand for appointments has its advantages, but eventually it creates a sensation of emptiness, of vindictive sadness. (*16 September*)

***

Philolaus propounds that "harmony is the unification of the composed multiple and the chord of the discordant". I propound: harmony is the unification of the multiple thanks to the chord of the discordant. To see the obvious *behind* the visible. (*21 September*)

***

In the restaurant Aki. I arrived half an hour early, and I used it to relax, to think about the mess I got myself into, and ideas, more antiseptic than sceptic, on the fantastic and dreams (the fantastic is, in a nutshell, the addition of the weariness of rationalism and the summary of the dreams and aspirations of humanity. Dreams don't make any sense – I almost agree – and are a theatre of perplexities and anxiety). Behind those quite boring ideas, a nostalgia for the marvellous non-reality hides, and an oblique melancholy clothed in erudite enthusiasm. (*23 September*)

***

Meeting of the Circle of Belleville. Without an imposed theme and in the end, without a theme at all. A meeting of old friends and friends of old. Around Jules Verne and secret societies (as ours is a little bit). (*27 September*)

***

I continued reading Michel Lamy's lucubrations on the esotericism of Jules Verne. Though it's certain that *Hypnerotomachia Poliphili* is a conspiracy, a plot around language, my film based on the book, *Love torn in a dream* is a conspiracy of stories. Stories – archetypes that are united against the unique history. Stories like plants in a garden of archetypical fictions. An English garden, Novalis' paradise. (*3 October*)

***

In the *New York Times*, there's a note on Philip Roth's latest novel, which is an uchronia: Lindbergh, in fact pro-Nazi, is the president of the US and an ally of the Third Reich. For me who make uchronias, I can't stop being interested in other uchronias. In reality, all fictions are. (*4 October*)

***

[*Klimt*]. Strange life. I can't complain about it. I can't love it. I can't say "it can't be", because it is. I am achieving everything I always wanted. To film fictions in countries which the authors I love come from. (*4 October*)

***

Rheomode: a cat is chasing a mouse. In normal language there are three elements: cat-mouse-chasing. The rheomode consists of encompassing the three elements in one single process (David Bohm). (*7 October*)

***

Thinking about the implicit order (the rheomode) and its relation to cinema. "Cinema is the art of turning the reversible into the irreversible using rheomodes." The rheomode, the de-equalisation of facts apparently articulated, like a cat chasing a mouse. Cinema is my cloudy mirror. (*13 October*)

***

The film [*Klimt*], after the cuts, lasts the duration it had to last, but the holistic function, the rheomode, went to hell. But what is certain is that now it is more explanatory, more narrative and still defendable. [...] It's strange that Arno, each time I explain to him how I'm going to do a scene, says: "Oh! This is the artistic part, let's talk about action and emotions". Surely he knows that I'm not a commercial filmmaker. And in a certain way, he wants it that way. (*14 October*)

***

I worked hard all morning. Nausea and sadness. I don't feel like making the film. Desire in our countries is important. Lunch with Valeria and [François] Margolin. Sadness, always sadness. And some oysters at the airport. Life itself. Or death. Ouch! (*19 October*)

***

I added several elements, but not as many as Arno would have liked. I am not sentimental and decency paralyses me. (*20 October*)

***

Last night, long conversation with Valeria about the work plans which are overloaded. At lunch time, with Emilio, we went back to re-examining the question set out by Wittgenstein in the *Tractatus*: what is said (the logic) and what is shown (the mystic). There should be a mystic art in which the showing predominates and a logic art in which the logical articulation and the recursive paradigm predominate. (*27 October*)

***

3.30 pm on a cloudy day. We had a simple lunch, Valeria and I. I'll go for a walk later. Music and reading. The life of a retired pensioner. Walked around the neighbourhood. Sunny afternoon. Good siesta. I bought some records: Mozart chamber music, works for clarinet, Bach, Paul McCartney. At La Locandiera, as usual, few people. The manager, always friendly. (*30 October*)

What does it mean, to expand the rheomode in indistinct or diffused cycles? To destabilise the frequencies of transformation so as to take them to interweaving vicious cycles. I shall go back on that. (*7 November*)

***

In the reflection of the windows I see an old gentleman, un *boeuf*, as they say in France, and it's me. Teillier, years ago, used to distinguish between the tame, trained mirrors and the wild mirrors, that catch you off-guard (...). Yesterday Philippe de Broca died, whom I had met (seen) in Montreal. We had dinner together, joked and laughed. He had many projects. He had asked about the availability of Agnès Jaoui. He seemed in perfect health. Cancer. We all live on borrowed time. Did he know? Didn't he know? He died filming. Fritz Lang died at 88. Not filming. Philippe was 71 (to me he'd said 72). (*28 November*)

***

Reading the interviews of directors of film noirs. The little set ups, the ploys. Nothing particularly sleazy. Only a little sad. Mechanical practice without poetry. But entertaining. Cinema hasn't changed. It has limited itself to Americanise. (*28 November*)

***

All sorts of strange symptoms: mild nausea for the last six months. And a kind of joy and serenity (*relief?*). At this point in my life I'm still in the middle of everything, working and inventing. (*3 December*)

***

[*Klimt*]. It's been a year and a half of preparation and I feel completely lacking in certainties. Everything is uncertain. When I made *Time Regained* I never felt unsure. Of course I sensed people's curiosity: what can that Chilean have to do with Proust? But in France, every human being *is* French until proof is offered to the contrary. And many foreign artists were mistaken and believed they had "succeeded" or triumphed while they were simply considered human. (*31 December*)

2005

Still reading Bohm and his defenders (Briggs and Peat)[29]. Cinema would be a language in which they are only verbs. A holographic weave that is obtained with combining *relevated* segments connected to other elements integrated in other sequences. The rheomode in cinema is obtained by coordinating dynamic relationships between separated fragments in various durations that *tend* to merge, outside the finished process that is the film, in other proliferating films. (*22 March*)

***

Some themes that I haven't touched for a while: 1) The landscape as protagonist. 2) The correspondence of the worlds (the other and this one), as in Swedenborg. 3) The ambiguity of the master-servant relationships. (*28 March*)

***

The rheomode continues to make my head spin. That language which favours the process and tries to eliminate all form of analysis, of fragmentation, is enough to leave one baffled. (*21 April*)

***

Summing up Bohm: the universe is a fluid, a river, from which emerge forms that our senses perceive as static, but which are in constant motion. Just like if we examine the currents of the river, we see whirlpools that seem independent from the river, thus we perceive tables, chairs, trees. (*23 April*)

***

Reading Jacques Gernet's book on Wang Fuzhi [*La raison des choses*], which is one of the most stimulating on Chinese philosophy and language. Much information on the way to use the *I ching* as a philosophical tool. Extraordinary similarity between the intuitive leaps of Chinese philosophy from the 17th century and David Bohm's discoveries. Zhang Zai: "All the things of this world are only transitory

---

[29] It refers to the physicists John P. Briggs and F. David Peat, the authors of *Looking Glass Universe: The Emerging Science of Wholeness* (1991).

bodies, formed by an 'assemblage' of energy". At the end of the day, my subject. (*24 April*)

***

In café Beaubourg, meeting with Paulo Branco at 4 p.m. to prepare *Orlac's Hands*. We talked about old times, creative freedom and other things. (*26 April*)

***

I started to play with the idea of making a film on animals, between Gautier – *Ménagerie intime* – and Sheldrake's hypotheses. Some twenty years ago, I remember, I wanted to make a botanical fiction, *Richard III* with plants. How to put together a film that favours the rheomode? (*1 May*)

***

In the processing of *Nerval ou le rêve de la vie*, I recognise various personal experiences: the difficulty to identify, in the past, what I've experienced from what I've dreamed and (the text's short on that) what I've imagined. It makes me think of the ideas of Pribram and Bohm. Let's say: "What I've lived, filmed or imagined". In times of war, for example, "lived" would be said "fought": "of what I saw and found in the fighting". (*14 May*)

***

In the bookshop Le Livre à Venir, I found a book that I read assiduously in Chile: Karl Jaspers's *Strindberg and Van Gogh: An Attempt of a Pathographic Analysis with Reference to Parallel cases of Swedenborg and Hölderlin.* (*15 May*)

***

I read again the first chapter of *Strindberg and Van Gogh*. As with many re-readings, my first impression came back to me. What impression? It is not that it made a big impression on me, but it was like the first reading and generated the same critical appreciation: everything that is said here about Strindberg's madness can be applied to me, only that, he had to live in a hostile milieu, surrounded by people reproaching him for one thing and its opposite. The same criticisms that were directed at him, I make about myself: lack of will, of tenacity, of talent, of imagination. I remember that as an adolescent, when I read the book, I said to myself that if he was mad, then I was too. An observation on Strindberg's relation with other schizophrenics (he never took them seriously): "We don't know of any schizophrenic who founded a cult that was followed by other schizophrenics". Only normal people follow him. What to think of the fact (if it is certain) that madness is an extreme degree and that that extreme demands normality to express itself? (*16 May*)

***

I've just been informed by Valeria that Le domaine perdu has been rejected by the Locarno Festival (after Berlin and Cannes in all sections, which I struggle to understand, because it is one of the films I am the most happy with). I suppose it is the way of filming, full of "allusions" and references. Anyway, it hurts. Valeria told me: "What do you want? You are quite old now", which hurt me even more. But it's good to know that "lone I muse but feel not lonely..." (Lope de Vega). (*17 May*)

***

As I'm figuring out the consequences of the rheomode in the cinematic process, I'm modifying the relations with my theory of the actors' work, favouring the connections within the groups and reducing the work of the character isolated from the others. How many characters are there in the vortex that is a character? How many masks? What is the process that modifies the appearance/disappearance of the masks? (*28 May*)

***

Le domaine perdu has been taken off in big cinemas. Few spectators. Nothing to be done: in France, my films don't interest many people. But I persist. (*14 June*)

***

I read a treatise by Jacques Lecouteux on shamanic journeys and out-of-the-body experiences. I am in the last chapter of *Mademoiselle Christine*[30]. Many ideas crammed in my head. 1)The whole film must be done according to the principle of "double vision". What we see must

[30] Later *Nucingen Haus* (2008).

be daily life according to the rules of verisimilitude, of wakefulness and, at the same time, dreamy, strange, improbable. 2) Superimposition of narrative strata. Polyfiction. 3) Dream dreamed by many. 4) In the last scenes, the dialogues are almost like theatre of the absurd. We must think Horacio Quiroga, Felisberto Hernández. Macedonio Fernández: *Not everything is waking life when one has his eyes open.* (*18 July*)

***

In the morning, long discussion with J.-L. Rivière on theatre-cinema relations or what he prefers to call «the conspiracy against theatre» (psychoanalysis and cinema). The opposition to facing the audience invented by the first stagings of the 20th century (1900, Max Reinhart) is achieved by cinema (not looking at the camera) and psychoanalysis (turning one's back on the interlocutor). But we are not talking about real presence. (*7 August as the song says*)

***

Planning the finances for the three years ahead and preparing for the inevitable retirement.
A few days ago, Andrés Claro arrived and said to me out of the blue: "We've lost the war". What war, I thought. I haven't seen any battle. But there's a persistent feeling of defeat nevertheless. "Persistent" is the word. All persists. Nothing exists. (*23 August*)

***

Each day it's more distressing to travel. And to live. But I can't complain because I feel good. Which in itself is also distressing. (*28 September*)

***

My General Theory of Cinema: Is cinema an inanimate object? It's obvious, even though the celluloid has been made with organic material. But its evocative capacity turns it into an *offsetting* for the dynamics of the spectator's imaginary. The film is reflected in the imaginary and changes in a to-and-fro motion. At a certain point we can say that the film looks at the spectator and looks at itself in its imaginary, creating an *imagining land*. Each spectator sees a different film.
The imagining lands animate symbols. The *imagen* of the classical art of memory is fixative of the text. What are the conditions for an imagining land to be activated? Before anything else, the use of *priming* (the

implicit memory). Thanks to the activation of the implicit memory (which, let's not forget, resides in another part of the brain than voluntary memory and specifies it) we can obtain an effect of emotional recognition (anagnorisis) of the facts. The image in cinema shows what is implicit in what is seen. By examining the relation, we will see things that are not obvious. (*29 September*)

***

For Raymond Roussel, every work of art was measured by its lack of correspondence with reality. Any relation to reality, the most unanimous truth, in the sense of direct correspondence with the facts of present or past life, will render it irreversibly ugly. What if life was a work of art? (This was the case with Raymond Roussel and Oscar Wilde.) Eccentricity is a way out of the horrible everyday. (*3 December*)

2006

In two more days I will have finished the bulk of *Lapidatio*[31]. Between Roussel and Singer. From Roussel I have used above all his way of attacking a story (which is not yet guessed) with word games or, in my case, with images and objects, and gradually giving meaning to the arbitrary elements, creating bridges by means of micro-fictions, in order, in the end, to let abruptly surface, as evidence, the fiction that encompasses everything (the extensive subtotal that emerges from the holonomy). (*13 March*)

***

Conversation with Emilio [Del Solar]: What if memories lived in a permanent present and we, by remembering them, made them come to our permanent past from the flow we call the present? Because to live is to pass and to remember immediate facts is to make them pass, thanks to recollecting, from eternal facts (but lived at least once) to a

88

---

[31] Script of a film from the writings of Raymond Roussel, never made.

prediction – bets of the will – and thus, charged with chronomorphic energy, to establish them in a new recollectable eternity. (*22 March*)

***

Idea for a film around the following theme: memories are eternal, the present is illusory. The cosmic river carries and brings images of the memory. (*18 April*)

***

Artist life, wandering life, sad life. *Tristitia* (sadness) and death. Well, that's how it is. Valeria puts up with it, and I drift off. And all dies a little. Error of [Alvaro] Covacevich[32]. (*1 June*)

***

Today I read the foreword to Tatarkiewicz's works by Bohdan Dziemidok. He examines his main ideas. The three levels of aesthetic experience: 1) sensual experience, 2) literary (that is, analytical, reasonable) experience, 3) poetic experience, experience of ecstasy and shock. Tatarkiewicz denies the separation between great and mediocre works, between a play and its mechanical reproduction on television. And here it becomes debatable, but his oblique way of detecting «middle ground» through a «relationist» practice is very stimulating. (*11 June*)

***

My [...] impression is that there is a separation, a *cleavage* between humanities and sciences, due for a major part to the submission of human sciences to sociology. Cinema is seen before all else as a symptom, a *comoedia mundi*. In France, we are gradually reaching the same thing. In *Positif,* two months ago, there was a commentary on the works of Zizek, in which the emphasis was placed on the *speculum*, theatre of the world. (*16 June*)

***

All of a sudden I realise that my project from a "theatre" (miscellany) that I know well, *Libro de buen amor (The Book of Good Love)* [Juan Ruiz], I've already made it in another way. Almanac or reader, or, as it wishes to be called, *Cofralandes* it is. (*16 June*)

89

---

[32] Chilean filmmaker, author of the film, *Morir un poco* (1966).

2007

What is it that attracts me in the miscellany game – Zapata, Timoneda, *Libro de buen amor*? The theatrical aspect of the world, the *speculum* dimension, the dispersion. Also the *collage*, sometimes close to the exquisite corpse. But aren't some of Breton's books miscellanies, as well as Macedonio Fernández's *The Museum of Eterna's Novel*? In fact, when I speak of miscellany, I am alluding to the heuristic process that consists of provoking the appearance of images through the combination of theoretical games and fiction in the form of a story. In the story, disbelief (Coleridge) is suspended. In the plot made of theory, credulity is suspended and «Plato's reason» is brought into play. (*22 February*)

***

The Life of Others, a classic, but accomplished film on the Stasi and its methods for controlling the country. Good use of the structure in three acts quite similar to that developed and expounded by Ibsen. An inflexible police officer with convictions, overbearing, overwhelmed with communist ideals: socialism and torture. Gradually his ideals burst, punctured by small incidents. Above all by the sentimental memory of a communist childhood, the recollection of Brecht's poetry, of Eisler's music. The tacit confrontation with the guarded and persecuted poet. What's new: the conflict is not explicit and never loses its metaphorical richness. (*10 March*)

***

Structure and order. According to the second principle of the independence of the shots, one has to consider that each function of the shots operates according to a different order. *Centrifugal function*: the frames operate according to classic rules: order, events, whether similar according to their growing or waning similarity. But also to the submission or the distancing *from* or *to* a given narrative model (the story that is told). The narrative model is the macro-story. For example: an earthquake is threatening (macro-story) and a group, a *sample* of characters, of individual destinies, weave and unravel a fabric of events that separate *from* or converge *in* the narrative model. At the level of sequences, the shots are distributed in a way that they operate subjected to the nondescript story. We have therefore a set of contained subtotalities in a "diffused totality" (because the earthquake will affect many more than the individual destinies). Those shots subjected to the criterium of the centrifugal order are given as belonging to a unique possible order: that of the film that we are seeing. Arranged according to a criterium of narrative efficiency (the best possible order according to the *enargeia*). The *centripetal function* brings us to arrange the shots from their edges and from there, "towards the inside". Each shot is an independent subtotal of the sum of centrifugal shots. To describe them, we can use the metaphor of the *vortex*, or whirlpool in a still river (a circular river that bites its tail, like in the hypothesis of Gold and Bondi), but in that river extensible totalities, a whole world, an entire life can exist. Think about Poe's *Manuscript found in a bottle*: a boat slowly swallowed up by a whirlpool, in the indifference of the victims. (*19 May*)

***

I leafed through a manga book (the Japanese comics), a visual montage that surprises me. The geometry and abundance of long shots. Suddenly it came to me that that system could be used for the staging of *Night across the street*. (*4 June*)

***

Today I finished (let's say I put the word FIN) the script of *Nucingen House*, ex *Mademoiselle Christine*. I'm always surprised when I write the last pages of a script to realise that I didn't imagine such an ending a few hours ago, a few minutes ago even, before writing the word FIN. (*7 July*)

***

In the airport, waiting to embark for Antofagasta. A little while ago I bumped into the ex-president Frei and his wife. He joked, saying: "Isn't it the most important film maker of Chile". And his wife added: "It produces antibodies". (*9 August*)

***

«cultural models» is a project I will discuss tomorrow with Andrés Claro. The starting point is: a hypothesis that has been disproved in one field (physics, for example) may be adequate if applied to another field of culture («substitution progress» to the avant-garde). This is the case with the Gold-Bondi hypothesis. It is also what happens with Ribot's theories that survive in the Stanislavski Method or [–]'s hypotheses of vision by snapshots, in the model of cinema as order created according to the logic of discontinuity and diffraction. Another theme is the fictional-fictionalised articulation of theories. The method of interweaving theories, which is understanding theory as a journey. An incomplete and mentally completed journey and vice versa. Yet another method is that of theory as a metaphor for another theory that is supposed to be known and/or forgotten, even if it is a voluntary forgetting. The notion (notions) of order underlies all these varieties. (*15 August*)

2008

Simon Leys quotes Chekhov noting that if in a play there is a revolver on the table in the first act, someone will use it in the third. And then he quotes Sartre, who observed at the end of a film screening, in which no detail escaped the control of the staging, that in the street, everything is left to chance. An idea: at the beginning a revolver and at the end a slightly smaller one. (*13 May*)

***

Forms of erratic narrative. I remember that a Peruvian professor (Oviedo), after seeing *Three Sad Tigers*, said: "Erratic, but interes-ting". It gave me the feeling that he was signalling a mistake there: wandering, that shifting of filmed acts that move without direction or destination point, in which "(it's the) walking (that) creates the path"[33]. Today we could say: "a narrative in which the generative order prevails". (*24 May*)

---

[33] '*se hace camino al andar*' alludes to a poem by Antonio Machado.

***

Today I was told that *Nucingen House* hasn't been accepted at the Venice Festival. Little by little they are marginalising me. But I persist in resisting the Unesco-Benetton cinema. In the afternoon I shall film another five or six pages. The fight is unequal. (*29 July*)

***

I read three novels that Antoine Beau suggested to me. I chose one: *Sur un air de Navarro*. There are entertaining things happening (car chases, etc.). Simon Leys makes a variation on the bad readings of a film. It seems that Julien Green, incapable of understanding the film that they projected, made up stories that mixed with the story of the scriptwriter. And that he witnessed projections during the colonial period in Africa in which, using the silent images of American films, the spectators invented stories in which, for example, the Black porter of the hotel who appeared for a minute, morphed into the demigod hero of the film story, while Clark Gable was reduced to the role of an extra. Could I use this situation as a starting point for *Sueño de una noche de verano*? (*13 August*)

***

I thought of writing a "plausible" autobiography, in which almost nothing is certain but nothing is implausible either. A little like the film *Klimt*, in which most events didn't actually take place. Possible title: *Portrait of the precocious artist as a sly old fox*. All that came to mind when I was going over the poems that I wrote, around five hundred, among them a few things that are not bad. And I saw myself in a viable life in which my main activity would have been literary, like a poet or a novelist. Or nothing at all. (*26 September*)

***

Notes for a film called *Annus horribilis*. It is a documentary around a year in the life of a film maker (myself). Wandering and experiences roaming all over the world in the middle of crises, family tragedies and many ups and downs. "A certain filming". To culminate in a project for a film called *Tres actos*. This year (2008) started badly for me and for almost all my friends. Believing in the "terrible aspect" of a year is giving too much importance to cycles. (*25 November*)

2009

I turned 68, a period of springs and autumns, a *shi* (Chinese scholar) would say. No chicha[34] and no lemonade. Too old to go back or to go far. Too little time here to close my eyes and let myself be carried by the bankless river. To read and write in this summer morning with no sun or rain, I opened the box that contains the red garment they gave me during my first stay in Japan, the red, the colour of the over 60s, and I put it on my lap. I read Chinese and Jewish texts. (*25 July*)

***

Good resolutions for my 68th birthday: 1) Walk more and do gymnastics. 2) Drink the same or less. 3) Think less about the past and more about the present to come. 4)Take more care of Valeria. 5) Tidy the books. 6) Prepare my classes better. 7) Film more with my digital cameras. 8) Organise more meetings with the Circle of Belleville. 9) To the body what belongs to the body, to the soul what belongs to the soul. 10) Get rid of hard feelings and make them laughable. 11) Reread Moore. 12) See more films. 13) Modify the introspections. 14) Clean the *mental dome*. 15) Reread Couturat. 16) Put into practice the following principle: "Intelligence, like the shameful parts of the body, must always be hidden, except in places conceived for hygiene and sport: universities and bathrooms". 17) Read less, study more. 18) Forgive the intellectual errors and aberrations of my fellow men. Correct my own and laugh about them. 19) As Strauss's waltz (*The bat*) goes: "Happy is he who forgets". 20) More haste, less speed. (*26 July*)

***

Private pantheon of stories and novels: *René Leys* (Victor Segalen) – *The Fox in the Attic* (Richard Hughes) – *While I lay dying* (William Faulkner) – *Other Voices, Other Rooms* (Truman Capote) – *Malpertuis* (Jean Ray) – *Ciau Masino* (Cesare Pavese) – *Uncle Silas* (Sheridan Le Fanu) – *The late Matias Pascal* (Pirandello) – *Tales of Moonlight and*

94

---

[34] A drink from the Andean regions.

Rain (Akinari) – *Bug-Jargal* (Victor Hugo) – *Ménagerie intime* (Théophile Gautier) – *El cocodrilo* (Felisberto Hernández) – *The Eternal Husband* (Dostoevsky) – *Sanin* (Artsybashev) – *Seven Gothic Tales* (Karen Blixen) – *The Book of Disquietude* (Fernando Pessoa) – *The Man who was Thursday* (Chesterton). (*2 August*)

***

In his essay "Is the Visual World a Grand Illusion?", Alva Noë introduces the notion of *amodal vision*, from which is extended the *amodal rhetorics*. Because of the imperfections of vision due to various factors, like the blind spots on the retina and its erratic roaming (four changes per second), the world that the eyes apprehend is discontinuous and, let's say, little reliable. But little reliable for whom? For what? This incredible disbelief implies a double vision, that of the perception supported by the rest of the body, essentially the hands and the pure visual perception which is, I think, a deliberate act, because it implies renouncing the "useful" vision. In cinema, the useful vision made us submit to the diktats of a narrative suggested by the images. And it brings us to leave aside the discontinuous vision that the voluntary operation of concentrating only on that which the eyes let us see, numbs, startles. The amodal vision, the illusion, is available there. And we can combine it with the discontinuity created by the juxtaposition of images (the appearance). We have here revisited the distinction between illusion and appearance. (*22 September*)

***

If, as Gide said, modern art (and its appendix: the postmodern) can be considered a vast enterprise of demolition, cinema, all cinema can be understood as an enterprise of reconstruction, or, if one prefers, a process of relaunching, or rebirth. That rebirth operates in parallel with the demolition. In that sense, one should consider cinema as a process distinct from the other arts. Cinema advances by going backwards, like river shrimps. *Cinema, an enlightened Jansenism.* (*22 September*)

***

"Voices of birds gathered in the old monastery/Shadows of birds passing over the cold fish pond." (Du Fu). The body map of a film.

The notion of finished and unfinished suggests the idea of the film as a finished body.

Predetermined. The unfinished film suggests the idea of phantom limbs that exist, move, hurt, even though they are absent from the film. But the film is not a body in the sense of an organism, though it tends to be. The finished film can be conceived as an imaginary map (of a still unknown territory), an old map of distant regions still unexplored. Another way to understand it is to imagine it as a territory in constant expansion. A corpus by *nature* unfinished. I conceive it as a double process: expansion and contraction. (*24 September*)

***

Reading chapter III ("The Range of Imagination") of David Bohm's book *On Creativity*. He quotes Owen Barfield, whom I heard of for the first time in the book *What Coleridge Thought*. Coleridge distinguishes between *primary imagination* and *fancy primary*: it is an act of creative perception, in which the images are fresher and more creative than derived from memory, and in which the *features* grow naturally and harmoniously as aspects of a totality made singular. And *fancy*, that consists in *putting together* images that in the memory are distant from one another. In cinema, this distinction can help to coordinate images perceived mechanically by the camera and their organisation (editing). (*Tuesday 6 October*)

***

At the airport. Before leaving I spoke to Valeria. A beautiful farewell sunset. Various readings and musics at these moments, it is as if various ages were merging and going around like wooden horses on a merry-go-round: 14 years, 70 years, 25 years, 8 years, 30 years. Different intensities overlapping and swirling. (*7 October*)

***

The character from the fiction *The wit of the staircase*[35] is going around my head. I can't get rid of it, like flies at the end of autumn. (*20 October*)
***

On music in cinema. Considering that cinematographic emotion depends on modifications of the duration (the immediate time) and that

---

[35] Novel by Ruiz published posthumously by Dis Voir in English in 2013.

the complexity of the tropes – in the chain of events – demands a strong adhesion, music is always superfluous. The immediate time is that aspect of the duration which village poets refer to when they say: "The moments are eternal (or endless)". In that temporality, it's almost amplifying the moments by means of the tension-relaxation between what didn't take place and the irruption of the breaks in the duration that abruptly modify the scene filmed. There are many films entirely made of the juxtapositions of scenes of that type (*tranches de vie*). But there are other films that flow smoothly and hover above the moments of life without pausing on any of them (*The Russian Ark*, *Citizen Kane*). In those in which there is a pause, it is allegorical, in the sense of "situations like that characterise those years". They are the films which use the time which the village poets refer to when they say: "but the years pass by". In those films, music is essential. Music, "which is pure time", telling us an abstract story that distils the flown-over facts. (*27 October*)

***

Yesterday, MRI scan. I stayed drowsy all day. Listening to Mozart's *Symphony n° 35*. It was the first Mozart symphony that I listened to attentively (some 50 times) when I was 14. I am still filled with wonder faced with the evidence of the composition, that feeling that the symphony was already there when Mozart composed it. What is that evidence? Not necessarily perfection or the classical ideal. Nothing to do with the sublime or with the harmony of spheres. What then? It could be that it is somewhat ineluctable, of an inevitable nature. There are works of art in which one goes from astonishment to astonishment (you and the author). There are others that were already there. In the first ones, the heuristic is explicit; in the others, it simply is not there. But regarding the heuristic, as I understand it, the word helps to show those phenomena that in the development of a work, marked the stages that brought it to a successful ending. But there are other phenomena that, at times, are organised by contradicting the facts that are arranged, taking the work towards its complete realisation. Contradicting and going against the current. They are going against the flow. Something like a "contrafactual" process. (*17 November*)

***

Reading Bolaño *[2666]*. A style occasionally made of "idioms", full of alliterations, rambling, but encompassing. Remember what Gide said about Stendhal: "He writes by stumbling." (*19 November*)

***

Reading Bolaño. How is it possible to generate the interest of so many readers with stories, surely full of details, that are about plots and the cheap cooking of literature, in which there is almost no elements among those called tricks or baits? And how can the writer think that such a book could generate interest to the point of insuring the financial security of his family after his death? And above all, why was he not wrong in thinking that? A first (temporary) answer would be the total absence of artifices, of set up. There are no twists or cramps in his language. The shiftings in time, the connected vessels, the circulatory system, are similar to the erratic conversations between friends. On top of that, there is the "imminent death" factor. I remember that when Manuel Silva[36] introduced me to Waldo Rojas in the Café Indianapolis, he said (to no one in particular): "I write like a man condemned". How do condemned men write? Apart from the fact that all of us, sooner or later, are condemned. It is not for posterity or for oneself. Maybe a "I admit that I haven't lived yet". A "I don't know" or an "Incensed, I withdraw" (as Mario Berríos had placed on his grave). (*20 November*)

2010

Using a Waterman pen for the first time, the exact replica of the one I had in Valparaiso in the 1950s. The ink doesn't go well with the paper of the notebook. So I go back to writing with my usual pen. Nostalgia weaves together images stirred up by a pencil, a plate of food, a scent or a song. There are networks fine like gossamer and very asymmetrical. They vibrate and swallow up present facts and use them to feed themselves. (*8 March*)

[36] Chilean poet, National Prize for Literature, 2016.

***

At which moment does *techné* begin to dominate and *manía*, the inspiration, take second place? And particularly, at which moment does the obsession with technifying the inspiration start to dominate the creative process? The techniques of meditating, the schools to teach to be by oneself, which takes the biscuit. And, by the way, is there a solitude, or is solitude gregarious? The idea that solitude is gregarious is in no way extravagant. I ended up thinking about Wittgenstein's strange statement according to which the unconscious doesn't have a "private property". It can't be appropriated, it is a common fund. (*9 March*)

***

I left the hospital somewhat dizzy because of the anaesthetics and the smells[37]. I found out that I won the prize for best director at San Sebastián[38]. I have here the speech for an actor to read: "Gentlemen, someone said 'all prizes are unfair', because films are complex individuals, deserving and lovable, and it's not fair arranging them from best to worse. That clarified, I'm especially grateful to the crew of actors and actresses without whose devotion this film perhaps would have been possible but not credible. I also think about the technical crew which knew how to put at the disposal of this film maker of another century the expressive possibilities of new technologies without losing anything of the old tricks. I'm thinking of Paulo Branco, etc. And finally, I thank the medical team of Dr Eduardo Barroso at the Curry Cabral hospital, illustrious heirs of Don Sebastián, the one who said: "Let's die, yes, but with a parsimonious slowness". Without them the film, literally, wouldn't have been possible. I keep up my sleeve other thanks for future prizes". (*25 September*)

***

Prize of the Critics at the São Paulo Festival[39]. Thanks: "I am grateful for this Prize of the Critics because it is a reward not only for what this film shows but also for what it conceals. For there's no pressure, you see, it doesn't coerce me to anything more than giving thanks. Because, though the representatives of cinematographic justice, the critics don't feel obliged to be blind. My friends know that I distrust prizes, because,

99

---

[37] Staying in Portugal, Ruiz had to undergo an urgent liver transplant.
[38] The San Sebastian International Film Festival awarded him the prize for his film *Mysteries of Lisbon* (2010).
[39] This prize was awarded by the Saô Paulo International Film Festival and he received it also for *Mysteries of Lisbon* (2010).

quoting Paul Valéry: "The free spirit abhors competitions. He senses that if defeats leave us disheartened, victories break us down". But don't be mistaken. I am very happy with this prize, because it gives me the opportunity to thank André Szankowski, Charles Saboga, script-writer, Valeria Sarmiento and Carlos Magdaleno, who did the editing. To Rosa Ruiz, my dear wife, to Adriana and Elena Sarmiento, my very dear friends, and to Fernando Pessoa, my *alter ego*. And to Domingo Caldas Barbosa, my favourite Brazilian musician, who never won prizes but harassment and abuse". (*3 November*)

2011

*P*reparing myself to attack the following projects: *Avatares del amor y de la infancia* (April), *Sinfonía Dante* (February-March), *The wit of the staircase* (tomorrow), correction and layout of a book of poems (120 poems), *Corazón de carne y hueso* and, of course, *El libro negro* (around the end of the year). There are other projects not well-defined, and with vague responses. For *Sinfonía Dante*: editing and projection of Barceló's drawings for 50 minutes. (*14 January*)

***

Reading *Ars combinatoria*. The whole can always be divisible in smaller wholes (*tota minora*), totalities thought as wholes that are part of bigger wholes and like that to God. And in that whole, it is possible to establish variations (*variatio*). But inasmuch as the variations in their combination can be considered a totality as such. Two types of variations exist: *variatio complexitas* and *situs*, variations of order. Let's take the fragment of a film: we have the way the parts are affected by their projection (of the frames) according to the frequency given for the division of the fragment in frames, and each frame in distinct spectres. Each spectre is in danger of transforming itself, inside the process of digression, in "spectral" migrations, in which each element of the spectre reconstructs, and disintegrates to and from other places (other frames). Of these migratory journeys, fake concretions are born that load and download the facts incarnated in each concretion. (*30 January*)

***

A terrible idea: Yenny Cáceres tells me that his fascination for Wagner's operas comes from his recollections of the film *Star Wars*. So I told him that Wagner evoked the Second World War for me, and not much else, that the few themes repeated obsessively reminded me more of Peter Lorre in *M*, as a sign of his criminal impulse. And, all of a sudden, the enlightenment: the Germans, warmonger people who incarnate "pure aggression", people keen on fairytales, were precisely the people who carried out the Holocaust, the Shoa. By doing so, they put into practice the idea that hides behind all fairytales: the destruction of the witch. And, in fact, didn't the Nazis claim they were the custodians of an occult knowledge?
Night across the street (the house that moves closer) is also the allegoric image of the imminent (and eminent) arrival of death. When the house moves closer, the toys in the room are snatched away. (*21 March*)

***

I read the texts of tribute that the members of the filming crew (of *Night across the street*) wrote me. All of them wish and manage to express an affection that baffles me and almost makes me feel embarrassed. They are not disproportionate praises, they are simple words from melancholic and grateful Chileans, grateful for what, I don't really know. It is no more than a small exercise book, in which each wrote a few lines of farewell. And here's the problem. I feel they are biding me farewell, mourning and missing me. Great consolation, though: the most modest members of the crew, the workers, costume designers, make-up artists and assistants, use the word "humble" as praise. Smile and simplicity. I don't see myself smiling or very humble, but it seems that they see me like that. All the better. (*1 May*)

***

I read an interview or conversation with Lihn and Schopf dating from 1970, 41 years ago[40]. Young theorists precariously seeing a future

[40] Enrique Lihn and Federico Schopf, "Diálogo con Raúl Ruiz", *Nueva Atenea. Revista de Ciencia, Arte y Literatura de la Universidad de Concepción*, n° 423, July-September 1970.

cinema that, without losing its complexity, would be possible within the socialism we were inventing. Spluttering of silly dogmatism appears here and there, but much is salvageable still. (*1 May*)

***

I take up this notebook again. Many things have happened in the meantime. Many deaths (fifteen?) but also many films that have come to light (twelve?). This morning I worked at correcting *Mostralia* (o *Aurora dorada*). I shall see again *The Red and the White*. I ended up regaining a little humility, which helps me to accept that I have much to learn from [Miklós] Jancsó. (*19 May*).

***

I had lunch with Emilio (del Solar) and we talked about a project to film philosophical dialogues and logical mimes. Themes for filmed dialogues: 1) Image and negation. 2) Pain and duration. 3) How can there be no sorrow in heaven? 4) The laughter of the gods. 5) Biography of concepts. 6) The present (Is this the present?). 7) The world is *All* that occurs. This Whole, does it also occur? In that case, the world is one of the occurrences that occur in the world. 8) The "esseism" of God. (*21 May*)

***

Reading *El alma y la voz de la naturaleza* (Lagunas). A stimulating idea: the words (at least the nouns) are always metaphors, whose comparability is direct, indirect or diffuse (or multiple). The metaphors that the classic notion of nature generates are structured by means of rectifications (tensors and expanders) that are themselves metaphors. That brings us to the theory of uncertainty that constitutes the substance of language itself. A is like B. The earth is like the water, the water is like the sky. Since A is like B, B is what it is. If we imagine each segment of language as a field, with its functions of attraction, repulsion and even "destruction", it gives us the world of language as a world dissolving and rebuilding itself, being born and dying, being reborn and expanding. (*26 May*)

***

My health hasn't changed. Light shortness of breath when I walk more than 200 metres without stopping, difficulty to swallow (dystonia), sore throat (mild) and reflux at night, cough after eating (it tends to lessen), sneezing (it tends to lessen), flatulences (stable), urine regular (three times a night), cold (tends to diminish), feeling of being hungover (variable), compulsive yawning at midday. (*30 May*)

***

Several observations around the story (the stories) that a segment of film can tell with its extensions and contractions. A man enters a house in ruins. Let's draw out in our imagination what he's going to do: Is he looking for something? Or entering without purpose, or, and it is more complex, several purposes are going to be aborted, one after another. The ruins, let's say, are fragments (in the sense that Edgar Wind gives them, that is, parts of optional totalities that struggle to emerge or escape). Let's accept the segmentation of the man's intentions (he was looking for a document or simply for a reason to enter the place). Let's imagine intentions that are, let say, directional, non-parallel and non-continuous arrows. Other characters see the man enter the place in ruins. Some feel the impulse to follow him, to spy on him. Let's imagine that group as ruins, in itself a ruin in movement. Let's pretend that these ruins are parts of incomplete sub-totalities whose incompleteness is provided with directionalities coherent among themselves. (5 July)[41]

[41] Last entry in the diary. Raúl Ruiz died in Paris on the 19th August 2011.

Printed in U.E

Meilleures Impressions - France